34
Alpujarras Walks

by

Charles Davis

Discovery Walking Guides Ltd

34 Alpujarras Walks

First published - March 2003
Copyright © 2003

Published by
Discovery Walking Guides Ltd
10 Tennyson Close, Northampton NN5 7HJ,
England

Maps
Maps are adapted from the **Alpujarras Tour &
Trail Map** (Super-Durable edition) published by
Discovery Walking Guides Ltd

Photographs
Photographs in this book were taken by the author,
Charles Davis, and by Jeanette Tallegas. (except
where indicated)

Front Cover Photographs
Mulhacéen (top) and La Mezquita (bottom)
Both provided by the author.

ISBN 1-899554-83-1

34 Alpujarras Walks

Contents

GR142 (one-way timings)

THE WESTERN ALPUJARRAS (return timings)

BARRANCO DE POQUEIRA (return timings)

LA TAHÁ (return timings)

THE AUTHOR

Charles Davis was born in London, and has lived and worked in the United States, Sudan, Turkey, Ivory Coast, Spain and France. With the onset of middle age, he realised that the urge to roam was better satisfied by walking than bouncing about on the back of a lorry in the middle of the desert, and now divides his time between mountain tops, desk-tops and laptops. He is the author of numerous highly praised and wholly unpublished novels.

Jeanette Tallegas has spent thirty odd years labouring for the French education system, from which she has finally, gleefully, taken early retirement. Asked what she intends doing now, she resolutely replies, "Nothing". Nonetheless, she does follow the author up various gruelling mountains, frequently alarming younger ramblers who seem to assume that remote and inaccessible places are the preserve of youth.

Bati is an Old English Sheepdog. He is large and shaggy and not overbright. However, he was sufficiently winsome to overcome the author's prejudice against pedigree dogs, and was consequently plucked from the Municipal Dog Pound where he had been dumped by his previous owners. Despite initial misgivings (he expressed a strong preference for staying in the car), he is now quite mad about mountains.

Charles and Bati

FOCUS & SCOPE

Situated in the south-east of Spain, the Alpujarras stretch from the high peaks of the Sierra Nevada to the shores of the Mediterranean and are defined to the West by the Lecrín Valley and to the East by the confluence of the Andarax and Nacimiento rivers. Resembling in the West the Pyrenees and in the East the high Atlas, they reflect in microcosm the Iberian peninsula's role as a tectonic, botanic, geological, and cultural buffer zone between Europe and Africa. They also provide some of the best walking in Europe's second most mountainous country.

This book describes walks in the High Alpujarras of Granada, traditionally the singular Alpujarra Alta or Nevedense. Some of the walks are well known, others less so, some are 'new'. Most are low to medium range mountain walks accessible to any averagely fit hill-walker. There is also a representative selection of the high peaks to the north, including the highest summit on the Spanish mainland, the Mulhacén. These high mountain walks call for more preparation and require a higher level of fitness, but they are all walks, and pose no technical problems. For those who've never been in high mountains before, the Alpujarras provide an ideal introduction. And if you just want to potter about and have a picnic, the 'Strolls' are designed to get you out of the car with maximum reward for minimum effort!

WHEN TO GO

There's good walking in the Alpujarras throughout the year, but there are one or two general observations that may influence when you choose to visit.

For the high peaks, **summer,** is the best time. But, if you're camping out, remember, even in Summer, the night-time temperature at 3000 metres can drop to zero, and conditions can always change suddenly and dramatically. Wind, in particular, can be a problem. If in doubt, turn back. Electric storms can be a problem in **September**.

At lower altitudes, the summer heat can make walking hard work, though there's generally a refreshing breeze at night. The Tahá de Pitres, GRs 7 & 142, and other low level walks from villages are best enjoyed in **spring and late autumn**.

In **winter** anything up to 2000 metres should be easy walking, even if you're above the snowline much of the time. Following the routes detailed here, the high mountains are still accessible (always presuming the weather is clear), but I wouldn't recommend them unless you or someone with you is used to winter walking at altitude. Conditions are generally most stable around **February**.

NB Despite the fun of the festivities, **Easter weekend** is not a good time to arrive in the Alpujarras. Every migrant and his dog is returning to the *pueblo* to expiate the sins accumulated in the city during the rest of the year, and the weight of traffic ploughing through Lanjarón suggests some biblical catastrophe has struck the plains. **August** is similarly crowded, though there are fewer foreign tourists and you may be tempted by the village festivals, one of which will have the mountains echoing to the thunder of firecrackers just about every evening.

GETTING THERE

The cheapest **flights** you'll find are probably to Málaga, but you may pick up some last minute bargains to Granada, especially during the ski season.

From Málaga, the easiest thing is to hire a car at the airport and drive east along the coast to Salobreña (E15/N340 direction Motril/Almería) then follow the Valle Lecrín (N323 direction Granada) north to the Lanjarón turning (A348) - a 90 minute to 2 hour drive. Otherwise, there's a daily **coach to Órgiva** from the central bus station (departure 3.30 p.m., return to Málaga 8.15 a.m.) and a more frequent service changing at Motril.

Buses **between Málaga and Granada** leave on the hour every hour between 7 a.m. and 9 p.m. except in the early afternoon when the times are 1.30/2.00/2.30.

Buses **from Granada to the Alpujarras** servicing most of the villages mentioned in this book (except Lanjarón, Cáñar, the lower Tahá de Pitres, Cádiar, Cástaras and Mecina-Bombarón) start at 10.30 a.m., 12.00 a.m. and 5.15 p.m.. As so often in Spain, time of arrival is a matter of considerable flexibility, but as a general guide it takes about an hour-and-a-half to reach Órgiva, two hours to reach the Poqueira Gorge, three hours to the Tahá de Pitres and Trevélez, four to Bérchules. The 10.30 bus terminates at Pitres. Granada, Órgiva, Cádiar and Mecina-Bombarón are linked by a separate bus service leaving Granada at 8.30 a.m. and 6 p.m.. Buses between Órgiva and Lanjarón run at 8.30 a.m., 10.30 a.m., 12 a.m., 1.30 p.m. and 5.45 p.m.. Buses **from the Alpujarras to Granada** start from Alcútar at 5 a.m. and 5 p.m., from Pitres at 3.30 p.m., and from Mecina-Bombarón at 6 a.m. and 4.30 p.m.

These timetables haven't changed in recent years, but it might be a good idea to check for up-to-date times on the Alsina Graells website (see Appendix C).

GETTING ABOUT

I have tried to work out a network of paths giving **access** to every walker, regardless of budget or means of transport. However, realistically speaking, unless you camp out overnight or are keen on insanely long days, you need a car to climb the higher peaks.

If you don't have a car, you can get from village to village on the GRs (see Walks 1- 9) or by the remarkably cheap bus service (see above) or taxis (see Appendix C), though the latter are not always to be relied on as it's entirely possible the driver might be busy tending his bar or digging his potatoes. Juan Funes and Fernando Vilchez (see Appendix C) are prepared to act as landrover taxis up to Walks 12, 13 & 14. Access to Walks 20 & 21 is possible via the Park Authority bus from Capileira. Where relevant (e.g. on linear walks), approximate departure times for buses back to the start point of a walk are given in the fact summary at the start of each itinerary.

If you are driving, don't forget the *pistas forestales* or forestry tracks (see Appendix A). They can be blocked by snow, landslides or excessive water, but if you fancy a day off from walking, they are an excellent way of exploring further afield and finding your own walks. Ask about conditions first. If you come to a stretch that you're not sure about, walk a hundred yards or so to get a feel for it. If you're not used to **driving off-road**, don't worry, cars are stronger than you think! Just make sure the tyres are fully pumped up and don't drive too fast - nor too slow, the vibrations can be terrible. But please slow down when you pass pedestrians. Even 10 km an hour can kick up a cloud of choking dust. The *pistas forestales* listed in the appendix are for driving or riding – I don't recommend walking on them.

THE WALKS

The walks described are within the capabilities of anyone who is moderately fit and used to hill-walking. However, don't be overambitious. Unless you're used to it, suddenly climbing a high mountain can be a deeply unpleasant experience – and coming down can be even worse! Build up slowly and, most importantly, measure your timing against mine on one of the shorter walks. Everybody has their own pace and you may need to adjust **walking times** accordingly. Also bear in mind that all pauses and breaks have been edited out of these timings. These are 'pure' walking times and only the super fit or the frankly deranged would do these walks in exactly these times. Allow at least fifteen minutes on top of every hour for path-finding, taking in views, catching your breath, eating, drinking &c. For longer walks allow even more time. The Mulhacén, for example, takes eight and a half hours, but you should allow up to twelve hours. Unless otherwise specified (e.g. on the GRs), all times include the return.

If you're not used to high mountains or long walks, don't be daunted by the **length** of these walks. On linear walks, you can always turn back when you're tired (there's no shame in 'not reaching the end'; this is walking for pleasure, not an Olympic event); and on circular walks, I have -where possible- included shorter versions for less strenuous circuits.

In the descriptions, I have tried to avoid excessive, distracting, and irrelevant detail, which tend to rob the walker of the pleasure of discovery - it also seems plain daft to stumble about a mountain with your face buried in a book describing what's around you. Nonetheless, tricky points are described in detail and I hope there's enough information both to keep you on track and enhance the experience. I have tried to avoid two common errors, making an essentially simple route sound like an expedition up the Matterhorn and, conversely, airily knocking off a 1000 metre descent in half a line. NB the number of words does not correspond to distance covered. A paragraph may detail a hundred yards, a line half a mile. It all depends on the complexity of the terrain.

I use the following **terms of reference**:

Dirt Track: anything a car can use, ranging from well-stabilised *pistas forestales* that are better than many Spanish roads, to the sort of routes that would put the wind up Colin Macrae.

Mule Trail: depending on how you look at it, a broad path or a narrow dirt track! Traditionally the law held that two mules each with two panniers should be able to pass side by side. Not all our mule trails meet this criteria (and it's entirely possible you will meet a mule carrying two bulging panniers), but they are all broader than the average path, usually follow ancient routes linking neighbouring villages, and are often roughly cobbled with rocks against erosion.

Path: a path is a path is a path, except when it's a...

Goat Track: which is a wilful sort of 'way' frequently disappearing and splintering into a confusing web calculated to baffle non-herbivorous bipeds.

For purposes of consistency (rather than a mere poverty of language), climbs are generally described as '*steep*', '*steady*', or '*gentle*'.

If you're leafing through the walk descriptions and find puzzling references to numbered pistas forestales or PFs, see Appendix A.

WAYMARKED PATHS

Waymarks in Spain tend to be a little wayward. You can usually rely on the red-and-white GR (*Gran Recorrido* in Spanish, *Grand Randonné* in French, possibly a *Great Ramble* in English! A long-distance footpath, in any case) markings, though don't be confused by similar marks on forestry tracks that have nothing to do with the GRs (a different system altogether cunningly waymarks equestrian/4WD routes with the same colours). In the text, capital *GR* indicates a path, lower-case *gr* a local road administered by the authorities in Granada. The yellow-and-white PR (*Pequeño Recorrido* or Short Walk) waymarks vary greatly. On some routes they're dotted about with wanton monotony, on others they're so rare they resemble an endangered species. As for the wayposts, they regularly disappear according to whether the local shepherd likes walkers or not. If the waymarking is good and likely to remain so, my description will be correspondingly brief. If the waymarking is haphazard or misleading, I won't mention it or will specify when our itinerary is different. Below are the conventional GR signs. Bear in mind that the paths are marked by local rambling groups, so there may be variations in the signs according to who marked the path.

= on trail
X off trail
≠ turning imminent (old waymarking system)
⌐ turning
⌐ turning

The **GR7** is the most famous waymarked route crossing the region and is described in detail in walks 1-7. It's an excellent introduction to mountain walking and an ideal way of linking the main villages of the region. Treating it as a 'commuting' path, I have on the whole left the GR7 itineraries as linear walks. However, not everyone will want to carry their kit from village to village or walk both ways in a day, so I've broken it up in such a way as to allow for a return to the starting point by bus. In addition, at the eastern edge of our map, there are two attractive strolls along the GR7 from Mecina-Bombarón to Golco and Golco down to the Río de Mecina (see Walk 7). To the west and going just beyond the limit of our map, is the GR7 between Lanjarón and Nigüelas, a monotonous walk, but an attractive if somewhat alarming drive.

The local authorities dub the **GR142** 'Between Peaks & Valleys'; 'Between Tarmac and Kindling' would be an equally valid name, since the path makers have displayed an uncanny affinity for asphalt and acres of desiccated retama just waiting for a brush fire. On top of that, it's perversely plotted and poorly waymarked (it sometimes seems like a DIY path, at other times the waymarkers apparently got tired of carrying the paint about and splashed it all over the place). However, it's not without its attractions, there's virtually nowhere in the Alpujarras without its attractions, even the GR142, and the sections covered in our itineraries (see Walks 6, 8, 9, 23, 24 and 25) include some of the prettiest paths in the region. But if I don't describe it, don't do it.

There are innumerable **PRs** in the region, though only half-a-dozen are officially recognised (see the Step by Step map mentioned in the bibliography). Don't be shy of trying out unofficial PRs. The official routes don't necessarily gain anything in clarity by being recognised and even if the waymarks disappear halfway round, following one of the unofficial routes can be a beguiling way of whiling away an afternoon. The waymarking system is the same as for the GRs except in yellow-and-white rather than red-and-white.

The other well known waymarked routes are the **coloured routes** laid out in the Poqueira Gorge. Most of these are covered by Walks 15-18, which is just as well as the wayposts frequently disappear and the pretty wooden map-boards dotted about the valley are also pretty useless, especially when they've been effaced, as is often the case. If you do happen to be using somebody else's map, beware of what should be a nice circuit from La Cebadilla up round the Río Toril. The path on the left bank got buried in a landslip several years ago and has yet to be repaired.

ACEQUIAS

No visit to the Alpujarras is complete without a walk along an *acequia* (see Walks 1/10/13/17/20/32/34). The *acequias* are a network of irrigation channels tapping the aquifers of the high mountain. Who first developed them is debatable, some authorities crediting the Moors, others the Romans. Either way, it had become a Moorish 'art' by the time Felipe II expelled the remaining Moslems after the rebellion of 1568, as he made one family in each village stay behind to show the new Christian settlers how the system worked.

Some *acequias* were hacked into cliff faces by masons suspended over vertiginous drops (beware of following *acequias* without taking a close look at the contour lines on the map), but most follow gentler contours and are more like ditches, dug into the hillside and reinforced by the skein of roots encouraged by filtration. Occasionally you will see an 'improved' version lined with PVC or concrete to prevent leakage, but not for long since the ground tends to dry out, the supporting vegetation dies, the undergrowth rots, and the whole lot falls apart.

Walking along *acequias* is a delight, but remember, these are still working paths. You may see an *acequero* with an adze fishing rocks from the water, clearing obstructions, rebuilding the wall... For him walking is a chore, not always a pleasure. It is, if possible, even more important than on 'ordinary' routes that we take care not to destroy the path. So beware of kicking rocks into watercourses and, if part of the buttressing looks weak, try and avoid it.

FLORA AND FAUNA

Details are beyond the scope both of this book and my expertise, but where relevant, likely sightings are mentioned in walk descriptions. Perhaps the two most emblematic animals are the mountain goat and the golden eagle. Also, at the right time of year and right altitude, you will probably see wild boar (steer clear if they've got a litter of cute little piglets with them), partridge, hoopoe, wasp-catchers, and any number of birds of prey. The most common trees (not counting plantations of pine) are holm oak, chestnut and ash. The ash are a narrow-leafed variety common to the region but strange to northern Europeans, who tend to mistake them for poplar. Frequent references are made in the text to *retama*, a broom-like shrub from the sweet pea family that's pretty well ubiquitous in Southern Spain. If you're not already familiar with it, you'll soon come to recognise its long, splay-tipped fronds speckled with yellow flowers in spring and summer. Other common or emblematic shrubs and herbs include caper, alyssum, rosemary, thyme, saxifrage, camomile, and more variety of broom than I'd care to name. Insects and flowers are too varied and, sometimes, too unique, to even begin cataloguing. See the Bibliography for relevant publications.

DOGS

Bolstering your ego with something big and slavering does not seem to be an Alpujarran habit. Dogs are either friendly or frightened, and frequently noisy. Experience and anecdotal evidence suggest you would be very unlucky indeed to have any unpleasant encounters.

ACCOMMODATION, CAMPING AND REFUGES

Accommodation in the Alpujarras is plentiful and, by English standards, cheap. Except for Christmas, Easter and sometimes August, you should have no trouble finding a room on the spot. For the foreigner, there's a bewildering variety of names advertising accommodation (*pension, hostal, hotel, posada, fonda, camas, habitaciones*), but the distinctions are too fine for consideration. On the whole, facilities are clean and basic, which is enough for most walkers. If you want something more sophisticated, there are self-catering apartments and *alojamientos* or *casas rurales* (don't get too excited if you see these last phrases translated as 'Country Houses'; these are not the sort of places you read about in dentists' waiting-rooms) and some more upmarket hotels in Lanjarón catering to the spa tourists. You could also try the Hotel Taray in Órgiva or the Alcazaba de Busquístar near Trevélez. See Appendix C for more details and pre-booking options.

The park authorities have quite liberal **regulations about camping** and once you're up in the mountains, nobody's going to question where you put your tent. However, you might be faced with a half-hearted attempt to move you on if you camp beside a dirt track or road within the park. Camping in **mobile homes and caravans** is also prohibited, however, small camping vans are generally tolerated, provided they're tucked out of sight, and the occupants **light no fires and leave no litter**.

Puente Palo (Pista Forestal 2, Walks 13 & 14) is an official **camping area** without services. There are fully equipped **campsites** at Órgiva, Pitres and Trevélez. The only **manned refuge** in the Alpujarras is the Poqueira (tel. 958 343 349, see Walks 20 & 21) above Capileira. Some guidebooks and maps still refer to the Felix Mendes despite the fact that it was knocked down several years ago. The following **unmanned refuges** are on or near the walks described in this book: Tello, Ventura, Caballo, Cebollar, Carihuela, Caldera. There has been talk of building a refuge above Trevélez near the end of Walk 28, but for the present it remains just that.

EATING AND DRINKING

The Aplujarran diet is a **meat** *(carne)* and potatoes affair and generally very good (for the palate if not the arteries). *Charcutería* is a speciality and enormous hams hang from every ceiling. Classic local dishes include various spiced and/or dried sausages (*chorizo, longaniza, salchichón*), black pudding (*morcilla*), broad beans fried with ham (*habas con jamón*), and any number of cuts of pork (*cerdo*), lamb (*cordero*), kid (*choto*), rabbit (*conejo*) and chicken (*pollo*), generally griddled (*a la plancha*), smothered in garlic (*ajillo*), or stewed in a casserole dish (*cazuela*). Beef is elderly veal (*ternera*) and not very exciting. *Lomo* is loin, usually pork, *chuletas* are chops, *bocadillos* are sandwiches, and *casero/a* indicates something home-made.

Doubtless by now, **vegetarians** will be feeling deeply depressed and have concluded they'd better bring their vitamin supplements with them. In which case, they'd be right. As in the rest of Spain, a 'vegetarian' dish is likely to be a plate of beans with a lump of dripping bacon lard melting all over it. And if you insist on something genuinely vegetarian, you'll probably get a sorry looking plate of peas and an even sorrier looking waiter. Apparently, vegetarian meals are available at *El Jardin* in Pitres and *Ibero Fusion* in Capileira. Also, *Ana* on Calle Cruz Alta in Altabéitar (see Walks 23 & 24) serves vegetarian lunches that are highly recommended by her neighbours. *La Fragua* in Trevélez has a vegetarian menu which, judging by their side-orders, should be good. Otherwise you could ask for a *revuelto* (eggs scrambled with vegetables of the season), *tortilla de patatas* (Spanish omelette), *escalibada* (not common in this area, but worth trying if you find it; a delicious mix of aubergines, peppers, onion and garlic, fried or baked, drenched in olive oil and served cold), *berenjenas fritas* (fried aubergine), *patatas a lo pobre* (sliced potatoes fried with garlic and peppers), or *sopa de ajo* (garlic soup) - and hope the chef has resisted the temptation to garnish it with a little cured ham! And don't get your hopes up about the *ensaladas mixtas*, which usually come with half a tin of tuna dumped on top of them.

Despite some trout fishing in local streams, the Alpujarras are not the obvious place for **fish** *(pescado)* **or seafood** (*mariscos*), though the ubiquitous salted cod (*bacalao*, as much the national dish as paella) is on most menus, and if you can't get down to one of the fish restaurants along the coast, you might like to try *boquerónes* (fresh anchovies), *calamares* (squid rings) or, their babies, *chipirónes*.

The **pudding** is not an art the Spanish have perfected and often entails a glossy card indicating all the factory-made ice-creams on offer. However, most places will have rice pudding (*arroz con leche*), cottage cheese with honey (*queso con miel*), crème caramel (*flan*), and an assortment of fresh and dried fruit.

Breakfast (*desayuno*) is equally unimaginative and generally means toasted (usually baguette-style) bread (*tostadas*) with - in descending order of interest - *tomate* (crushed garlic and tomato), *aceite* (olive oil), *mermelada* (jam), or *mantequilla* (butter, which is never as good as the oil).

As for **portions**, nouvelle cuisine is a concept alien to the Spanish temper and you might wish to order 1 for 2 rather than ending up face to face with a steaming pile of pork that would keep a family well-fed for a week. *Tapas* in this area are still frequently given free with a drink, rather than being a bought appetiser which they have become in most of Spain. *Raciónes* are larger portions of *tapas*, *platos combinados* a full single-course meal, and the *menu del día* provides a cheap three-course lunch.

Wine is cheap and generally cheerful. The locals drink *costa* which tastes like a bizarre blend of rosé, fortified sherry-like wine, and retsina. Some of it is absolutely vile (beware if someone proudly presents something they call 'wine' and are pleased to claim is 22° proof!), but at its best it goes down with dangerous ease. For good *costa*, try the butcher (*carnicería*) *El Molino* in Busquístar. Their *costa*, tapped from the barrel into your own bottle, is excellent. Vineyards can be visited in the Contraviessa.

Alhambra **beer** (*cerveza*) is not bad by Spanish standards, **shorts** are never short, *sol y sombra* is a kill-or-cure mixture of brandy and anisette often deemed necessary early in the morning (this may explain why the rest of breakfast is so pedestrian), and *carajillo* is the name given to the endearing Spanish habit of brightening up their coffee with a tot of brandy.

There are plenty of *fuentes* and springs in the low Alpujarras and, on the whole, the **water** is excellent – at altitude even the rivers aren't beyond the pale if you're really pushed. Still, it's best to have enough water with you if you don't want to risk picking up worms – there's a lot of grazing in the high pastures. Sometimes you'll see a *no potable* sign indicating the water is not for drinking, though this may simply mean the authorities don't test it and don't want to take any chances. There aren't many high-mountain springs in the Alpujarras, but in general, the usual rules pertain: if it comes directly out of the ground, preferably the rock, it's OK; if it runs on the surface or (most importantly) is still, it's not. Beware of leaving water bottles filled from the Fuentes Agrias in La Tahá standing too long; the iron and mineral traces here are so high they leave a deposit discolouring the inside of your bottle. These waters are also faintly gaseous – open a bottle that's been left for the night and you'll hear a faint pop!

Gallego remains the definitive guide to walking in Southern Spain, despite being a bit daunting in scope, detail and interminable cross-referencing. If you can read Spanish, his work provides an invaluable introduction to the many *sierras* of Andalusia.

The Alpinas map is up to their usual standard, but useful nonetheless, especially for local details and names other maps may ignore. With the occasional glaring exception, the IGN and military maps are generally good on nature, but not always so hot on what man has done to it. The Penibetica maps are easy to use but oversimplified and apparently premised on the assumption that you're Clark Kent. I have not found ANY previous map that does not include some inaccuracies.

Nevedensis in Pampaneira have a good stock of books about the region (mainly in Spanish) and can help with information about routes, weather conditions etc.

My thanks to numerous park rangers, shepherds, *acequeros* and the many *campesinos* who look on in bemused but delighted wonder at tourists doing for pleasure what generations have done to survive. Their occasionally mocking but almost invariably welcoming and helpful comments, are one of the great rewards of visiting these mountains.

Thanks to Jeannette for keeping up and keeping me going, and to Bati for giving his paw to a Guardia Civil at just the right moment.

Finally, thanks to David and Ros Brawn of Discovery Walking Guides for believing in an unpublished writer, for entrusting me with so much valuable equipment, and for suggesting this project.

Map adapted from the **Alpujarras Tour & Trail Map** (Super-Durable edition) published by **Discovery Walking Guides Ltd**

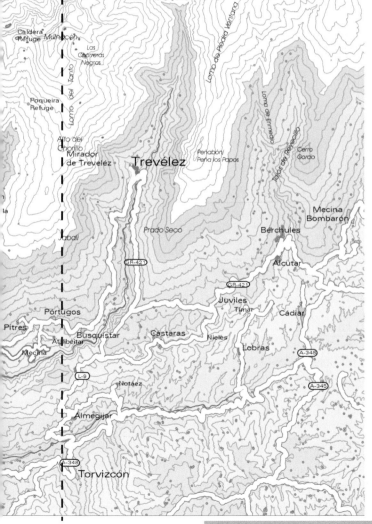

MAP NOTES

The map sections used in **34 Alpujarras Walks** are greyscale versions adapted from **Alpujarras Tour & Trail Map** (Super-Durable edition) published by Discovery Walking Guides Ltd. In the interests of clarity, not all waypoints referred to in the walk descriptions are shown on the map sections.

Alpujarras Tour & Trail Map is a 1:40,000 full colour topographical map covering all the regions explored by **34 Alpujarras Walks**. For more information on DWG publications write to Discovery Walking Guides Ltd, 10 Tennyson Close, Northampton NN5 7HJ, England or visit:

www.walking.demon.co.uk and **www.dwgwalking.co.uk**

"Tour & Trail" Legend, Legende

ROADS, TRACKS & TRAILS

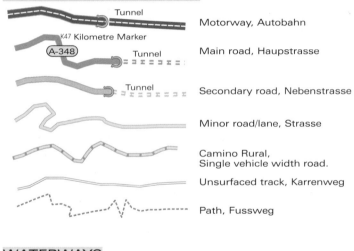

Tunnel	Motorway, Autobahn
K47 Kilometre Marker A-348 Tunnel	Main road, Haupstrasse
Tunnel	Secondary road, Nebenstrasse
	Minor road/lane, Strasse
	Camino Rural, Single vehicle width road.
	Unsurfaced track, Karrenweg
	Path, Fussweg

WATERWAYS

	River/Stream, Fluß/Strom
502m E. Embalse P. Presa	Reservoir, Wassertank

PUBLISHED WALKING ROUTES

optional route in green

Walking route, Wanderweg

GPS waypoint placed alongside route.

15🚶 34 Alpujarras Walks walking routes

• 486 △ 1,287

Height, Hohe, Altitud, Altitude

P. Pico/Puig   M. Montaña

HEIGHTS & ALTITUDE

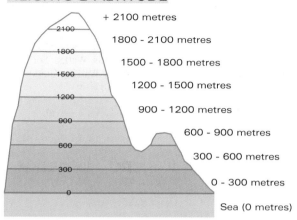

+ 2100 metres

1800 - 2100 metres

1500 - 1800 metres

1200 - 1500 metres

900 - 1200 metres

600 - 900 metres

300 - 600 metres

0 - 300 metres

Sea (0 metres)

 Marsh, Sumpf, Patano, Marais

GENERAL FEATURES

Lighthouse, Lechtturm   Mirador   Spring, Quelle   P Parking

Tower, Turm   Information   Historic Site   Helipad

Chapel, Kapelle   Hotel   Bar/Rest   GPS Waypoint

Football/Sports Ground   Picnic area, Rastplatz

Church, Kirche   Cemetery, Friedhof   Wind Turbine

Forest House   Camping   X Road closed to public access

34 Alpujarras Walks routes include GPS Waypoints. These refer to specific points along each walking route. A full GPS Waypoint list is provided for each walking route, although not all waypoints are shown on the maps. To use these GPS Waypoints, remember to set your **GPS datum** to **European 1979**. Using the wrong datum can result in significant errors in location.

GPS Waypoints are given in **Latitude/Longitude** coordinates; e.g. Walk 1 is Wp.1 36.55.2373N (Latitude) and 03.28.1498W (Longitude). When inputting the Waypoints to your GPS, do remember to have your GPS set to European 1979 datum.

GPS Waypoints are approximate positions, and while we quote positions to 0.0001 minutes of arc, in practice 0.0100 minutes of arc (10 metres) is an acceptable standard of accuracy. Note that on the map sections for each walk the GPS Waypoint symbol is placed alongside the walking route for clarity, not on the exact location to which it refers.

Waypoints alone are no substitute for an accurately written walk description, but will ensure that you know when you reach particular points in the walk description and that you are heading in approximately the right direction. Discovery Walking Guides are developing 'Personal Navigator Files' for all their new walking guide books, providing full GPS Track and Waypoint information for each walking route. These 'Personal Navigator Files' can be downloaded to your GPS receiver, via GPS software, so that you walk in the same footsteps as the author of the guide book. More information on 'Personal Navigator Files' is available on DWG's websites:
www.walking.demon.co.uk and **www.dwgwalking.co.uk**

- our rating for effort/exertion:
1 very easy   **2** easy
3 average   **4** energetic
5 strenuous

- approximate time to complete the walk (compare your times against ours early in a walk)

- approximate walking distance in kms

- approximate ascents/descents in metres

- from **0** (none available), up to **5** (exceptionalfood/drink/position)

1. GR7: LANJARÓN - CÁÑAR - SOPORTÚJAR

(Total time 3 hours 35 minutes)

Lanjarón – Cáñar:
This section of the GR7 gives a pleasant introduction to the contrasting landscapes of the Alpujarras, passing through well-irrigated, heavily domesticated land, barren pasture and an attractively wild valley. It's exposed though, so perhaps not ideal in summer.

(one way)

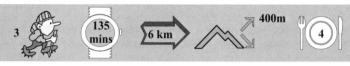

Buses back: none. The nearest taxi is Juan Funes (see Appendix C).

Leaving the car in one of the large lay-bys at the eastern end of **Lanjarón**, we follow the **A-348** to a newly restored house (**Wp.1**), 200 metres east of the **Río Lanjarón** bridge, fifty metres after the **Jamones Artisanos Morillas**. The GR7 starts on the stony path to the left of the house (NB NOT the main concrete track, the end of PF1 Branch C, just after the house. Waymarks on this concrete track are for the GR-142, not the GR7).

Behind the house, we take the narrow path climbing away from the GR-142 up to a dirt track behind an old metal water tank, where we bear right and then left onto a minor concrete track up to a modern house with a satellite dish on its fence (**Wp.2, 5M**). We then bear left and immediately turn right onto a wayposted path, which we follow up to a dirt track (**Wp.3, 10M**).

Fifteen metres to the left the path continues climbing, crossing the dirt track again (**Wp.4, 20M**) before rejoining it a few minutes later. We then stay on the track till a dead-end sign (**Wp.5, 30M**) and take the path on the left to follow a wide *acequia* for five minutes to another concrete track.

Turning right, we follow this track till we approach a major junction (PF1 Branch C/GR-142), thirty metres before which old GR markings on a rock to the right indicate a faint path on the left (**Wp.6, 40M**) heading towards the breeze block walls of a goat farm.

Following the path behind the farm brings us back to PF1 (**Wp.7, 50M**) just above a GR-142 signpost, where we cross PF1 onto a branch going east (**E**) and almost immediately come into sight of **Cáñar**. The track curves (**NE**) to a junction with another dirt track (**Wp.8, 60M**) on the right to the **Cortijo del Conde** (Walk 9, Wp.8). The GR7 continues on the left (**NE**) bearing left again at another junction (**Wp.9, 65M**).

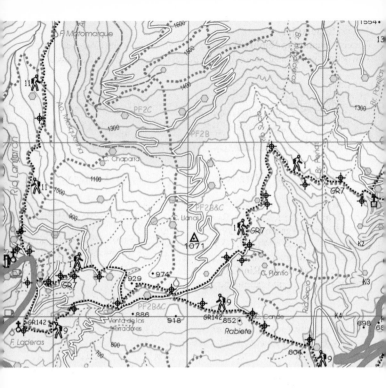

We leave the dirt track a couple of minutes later at two waypoints (**Wp.10, 67M**) to climb (**NNE**) across abandoned terraces before the path swings right (**N**) towards pine and fir, after which it descends a slightly precipitous stretch to cross a meagre torrent.

For the next thirty minutes, the path dips up and down, winding along a series of goat tracks toward the head of the valley, passing 20 metres below an abandoned *cortijo* (**Wp.11, 85M**) and then crossing a cluster of olive trees, in the middle of which it climbs very slightly to a waypost (**Wp.12, 89M**). It then continues in a northerly direction (**N**), winding up and down past oak, pine and fir, and eventually zigzags down to the **Río Sucio** (**Wp.13, 100M**).

Suggested Strolls	On the far side of river, a clearly waymarked path (not nearly so narrow and precipitous as it looks) climbs steeply and curves round the mountain to cross a patch of erosion (**Wp.14 120M**), just after which **Cáñar** comes back into view, some fifteen minutes away along a clear path crossing an *acequia* (**Wp.15, 130M**) and the road into **Cáñar** (**Wp.16**) before climbing up to the western side of the church.
From **Cáñar**, follow the GR7 west to **Wp.14**	
From **Cáñar**, follow the GR7 east to **Wp.18**	

Cáñar - Soportújar

The continuation to **Soportújar** is comparable to the previous section but with better views, easier walking and a perfect rest-stop at the **Río Chico**.

(one way)

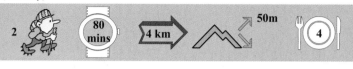

2   80 mins   4 km   50m   4

Soportújar - Órgiva (roughly) 4.15 / **Órgiva - Lanjarón** 5.45

From the *plaza* behind the church, we follow the **Calle Real** (on the left of the **Bar Mesa**) until it bears left next to a green metal door and descends to a concrete track (**Wp.17, 0M**), signposted 'Soportújar'. The track soon dwindles to a path that bears left (**N**) above the **Río Chico**, passing under shady walnut trees and below the **Cáñar** chestnut forest.

The path sometimes splinters confusingly, but all northerly traces eventually meet. Shortly after a stretch of more varied trees (acacia, poplar, eucalyptus) the path has been destroyed by a landslip (**Wp.18, 35M**). A way has been trodden by subsequent walkers but it can still be unstable, especially after rainfall, so take care. After the landslip the path is clear, soon reaching an idyllic glade at the **Río Chico** (**Wp.19 45M**).

> **Suggested Strolls**
>
> From **Soportújar**, follow the GR7 west to **Wp.21**
>
> **Soportújar** to **Carataunas** (**Wps. 24-25**)
>
> **Carataunas** to **Bayacas** (**Wps. 25-26**)
>
> **Bayacas** to **Órgiva** via the **Río Chico**

We then cross the river and descend the steps on the far side (**SSE**) to climb a slightly rough stretch where the path has been washed away and cut by tree-fall. Just after a stone bridge (**Wp.20, 50M**), ignore the narrow path climbing to the left and continue on the main path along the **Acequia de la Vega**, passing one short mildly vertiginous stretch and several ruined huts. (N.B. If you have the alarming sensation that the ground is giving way beneath your feet, don't worry! You're walking on a plastic irrigation pipe and the soil is sometimes thin.)

Ignoring a path climbing across the *acequia* to the left (**Wp.21, 65M**), we take the path below the *acequia*, passing a water-inspection hatch to descend between a stone wall and fields. The path soon bears left (**SE**), crossing another narrower *acequia* (**Wp.22, 70M**) and continues, descending between fields before bearing left after a small concrete-faced house (**Wp.23, 75M**) to join the concrete track into **Soportújar** (**Wp.24, 80M**) a few minutes later.

If you want to descend to Carataunas

If you want to descend to **Carataunas** (hotel/pension), **Bayacas** (rooms), or **Órgiva** (all services and GR-142), take the **Calle Estación** below the telephone booth beside the church then, just after the **Calle Xanfilla** sign, the

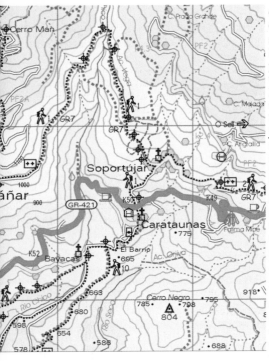

Calle Camino de Carataunas, which soon turns into a rock-laid mule trail. The path follows a terrace wall to pass between a house and a ruin, after which it dips down, bearing left at a junction before crossing an *acequia* and descending between 'La Rondilla' house and a *Telefónica* hut onto a concrete drive down to the road (**Wp.25, 12M** from **Soportújar**) 100 metres east of the **Montañero Hotel**, 300 metres east of the **Venta el Venao** (*comidas y camas*). To continue into the centre of the village, cross the road and take the path next to a wooden telegraph pole, which descends directly into **Carataunas** beside the church, fifteen minutes (**15M**) from **Soportújar**.

For Bayacas or Órgiva

For **Bayacas** or **Órgiva**, continue through **Carataunas** in the same direction and take the concrete lane below the car-park between the *Casa Consistorial* and the telephone booth. After eight minutes (**8M**), the lane joins a dirt track descending to the semi-abandoned hamlet of **El Barrio**. Follow the path through the hamlet to an *acequia* with a little concrete bridge with *puente* engraved on it (**Wp.26, 25M** from **Soportújar**). If you want a more scenic route, turn left here (see Walk 10, Wp.2). If you want to go to **Bayacas** or take the most direct route to **Órgiva**, continue straight ahead and turn left on the track descending along the **Río Chico** to the bridge into **Bayacas**, thirty minutes (**30M**) from **Soportújar**.

If you want to continue to **Órgiva**, stay on the left bank till the end of the eucalyptus trees. Cross the *acequia* onto a path below the escarpment that soon comes out on a dirt track above a concrete ford. Follow the track to the BP filling station at **Órgiva**, half-an-hour later.

2. GR7:
SOPORTÚJAR - PAMPANEIRA

A slightly irritating start (poor plotting, appalling waymarking), is redeemed by an attractive path passing pretty farm buildings, and is turned into a positive triumph by the food at the **Hostal Guillermo** (though not for vegetarians, I'm afraid). After **Wp.2** the path is well marked, though the waymarks are old. You can park at the eastern end of **Soportújar** or one hundred metres before **Wp.1**.

(one way)

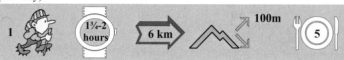

1 | 1¾-2 hours | 6 km | 100m | 5

Buses back: 4 p.m. / 6.30 p.m.

From the *plaza* in front of **Soportújar** church, we follow the road east (**E**) toward the GR-421 until a wayposted concrete path (**Wp.1, 5M**) leads up to the cemetery. Dropping down onto the dirt track below the cemetery, we turn left then bear right at the junction thirty metres later and, at the end of a recently built retaining wall, right again on an unmarked path. This path climbs past a large, empty reservoir (**Wp.2, 20M**) towards a line of pine where it joins the tarmac section of Pista Forestal 1 (**Wp.3, 25M**). We turn right and follow the tarmac till it bears due south, and then turn left on a wayposted dirt track (**Wp.4, 30M**). Shortly after the first left-hand bend we leave the dirt track and take a waymarked path on the right (**Wp.5, 34M**).

Suggested Strolls
Park 500 metres up Pista Forestal 2 and follow the GR7 east (**Wps. 3-6**)

The path becomes more attractive here, crossing a couple of torrents and passing a series of cabins and ruins before veering into the **Poqueira Gorge** where it descends towards the road and comes out on a dirt track (**Wp.6, 52M**). We turn right and climb a concrete driveway to recover the path on

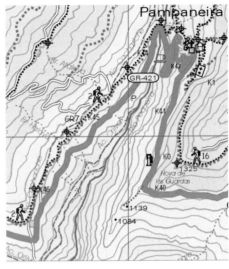

the left of two large metal gates.

A few minutes later, the path crosses another torrent and bears right to pass between a large cabin and a high terracing wall. After a few metres of slightly degraded path, we descend along the left branch of two rough *acequias*, then climb between two terraces and cross two more torrents to emerge below a small reservoir (**Wp.7, 65M**) after which the path climbs past more ruins and semi-abandoned huts to the first mulberry trees, announcing the proximity of the village.

The path dips and rises through mulberry, fig and chestnut trees and crosses another narrow torrent, before passing beneath a long concrete rampart (**Wp.8, 85M**) overlooking the **Hostal Guillermo** and the electricity installations of **Pampaneira**. It then gradually descends to the GR-421, which it follows across the bridge (**Wp.9, 95M**) over the **Río de Poqueira**, where we have two options.

For **Pampaneira** village, turn left 100 metres after the bridge onto a narrow path that crosses a dirt track and passes the *Estación Transformadora*, above which a narrow concrete lane (**Wp.10, 105M**) leads into the village. Alternatively, for excellent food (their black pudding is sublime) and a lovely shady terrace, stay on the road another 100 metres for the Hostal Guillermo.

3. GR7:
BUBÍON - PITRES - BUBÍON

Apart from one slightly monotonous stretch (after **Wp.5**) this is a nice linking path through varied vegetation with several opportunities for making your own itineraries (see the strolls and walks in 15, 17 and Pista Forestal 3). The alternative return route has particularly fine views of the **Tahá** villages and the **Sierras Mecina**, **Contraviessa** and **Lújar**. You can park just in front of **Wp.1**.

Timing: **Bubíon - Pitres** via GR7 (1 hour 20 mins), 4km (one way)
                 Alternative return 1 hour 10 mins (from **Capilerilla**)

Buses back (from **Pitres**) 3.30pm / 6pm (from **Bubíon**)
2.30pm / 7.45pm

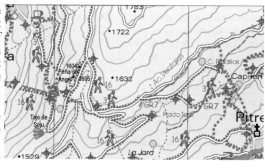

The path starts on the main road at the south of **Bubíon** where a G R 7 p o s t indicates, a little o p t i m i s t i c a l l y, 'Capilerilla 1h' (**Wp.1, 0M**). We follow the **Calle Ermita (S)**, ignoring a path to the left and continuing along a dirt track climbing from lower down in **Bubíon** which soon passes a horse corral with solid wooden gates, then bears left and begins winding uphill. When the main track bears left (**NE**) at a water-inspection hatch (**Wp.2, 13M**), we continue straight ahead on the narrower track, and one minute later turn right at a waypost onto a narrow path through oak trees.

This attractive, rocky path climbs steadily past occasional waymarks to a junction of paths (**Wp.3, 25M**) just below an electricity pylon and shortly before the water pipe descending to **Pampaneira** (see Walk 16). We bear left here to climb towards the rocky outcrop of the **Peña del Ángel**. The path goes under the electricity lines and passes a waymarked pylon before descending to a broad dirt track (**Wp.4, 35M** - see PF3 Tajo de Soju stroll) near some abandoned transformer towers.

Crossing the main dirt track, we take a minor track (**SE**) to descend through pine, fir and oak into the **Barranco de la Sangre**, so called for a bloody battle between Christians and Moors, after which the Christians claimed their blood flowed uphill to avoid mingling with that of the Moors! Ignoring a track on the right (a potential link to Walk 16 Wp.15), we cross the *barranco*, climbing on the eastern side to a junction of dirt tracks (**Wp.5, 45M** - see Walk 16), just above a 'graveyard' of concrete pipes. We cross the main *pista forestal* and take the track signposted 'Pitres/Capilerilla'.

We then bear right at a Y-junction and right again on a minor track (**Wp.6, 60M**) shortly before a meadow and field of saplings. Just before the chain closing this minor track to traffic, we turn left on a path that descends to join another rough dirt track (**Wp.7, 65M**) which soon dwindles to a path.

We follow this track/path past a stone signpost for 'Bubíon/Capileira', keeping the old metal fencing posts on our right and ignoring a branch on the right that passes stone cabins and a large chestnut tree. The path gets rougher as it descends toward a stand of poplars, where it bears left (**NE**) alongside an ancient retaining wall with pink crosses painted on it, before coming into **Capilerilla** beside a tall poplar and a waypost (**Wp.8, 75M**), 'Bubíon 5.5km / Pitres 0.5'.

Suggested Strolls
Capilerilla – Pitres (Wps. 8-9)
Capilerilla – Acequia de las Ventajas (Wps. 8-10-6-8)
Also see Pista Forestal 3

Continuing on the path into **Capilerilla**, we pass under a couple of *tinaos* (the terraces that turn streets into tunnels) and, one minute from **Wp.8** and immediately after the *ayuntamiento* noticeboard, turn right onto a concrete lamplit track passing underneath a house, after which it becomes a dirt path leading down to **Pitres (Wp.9, 80M)**.

Return To Bubíon

To return to **Bubíon** we take the narrow concrete lane on the left, a few metres east of the *ayuntamiento* noticeboard in **Capilerilla (0M)**. The lane climbs under a walnut tree and passes a house on the right, after which it turns into a dirt path climbing **NNW**, passing a hazelnut tree and a house gated with an old bedstead before bearing right towards a large chestnut tree and a water hut with a couple of meters mounted on its southern side.

The path then climbs steadily, passing another house and water hut till it crosses a branch of the **Acequia de las Ventajas (Wp.10, 10M)** beside a flimsy waypost for 'Capilerilla'. Ten metres below the *acequia*, on the far side of the tiny meadow with a walnut sapling, there's a nice picnic spot, a grassy platform under shady chestnut trees.

To continue the walk, we turn left at the *acequia* and follow the track leading away from the green metal gates. After passing above the meadow and saplings (chestnut interspersed with vines) seen from **Wp.6**, ignore the track descending to the left and climb briefly along the main track to rejoin the GR7 at **Wp.6**, ten minutes from the *acequia* (**20M**) and fifty minutes from **Bubíon**.

An attractive woodland route with fine views over the **Trevélez** gorge. Easy to follow and, for the most part, easy walking. Entomologists should head for the **Barranco de la Bina** where there's an incredible variety of insect life. Between the cemetery and **Wp.4** the way widens and narrows so often I'll not distinguish between mule-trails and paths, but stick to 'path' for simplicity's sake. Although it's not very steep, the route is riven with *barrancos* that have a certain remorseless quality to them. Every time you think you've finished climbing, you dip down into another *barranco* and scramble up the other side. For the GR7 between **Pitres** and **Busquístar**, see Walk 23. There's plenty of parking on the access road to **Busquístar**.

(N.B. If you're not using our map, beware. On most maps the stretch of the GR7 between **Wps. 9 & 11** is dramatically inaccurate.)

(one way)

4   *4 hours   9 km   500m   5

*(The official timing, 5 hours 30 mins, is accurate counting rest-stops)

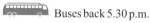 Buses back 5.30 p.m.

> **Suggested Strolls**
>
> Bearing left at the cemetery (**Wp.1**), follow the track till it peters out in a terrace. Drop down onto the next terrace and head east to a low cabin. Take the path down beyond the cabin to rejoin the GR7 (**Wp.2**) and return to the cemetery.

After crossing the main road opposite the entrance to **Busquístar**, we take the narrow dirt path (**Wp.1, 0M**) climbing past a house/byre to the cemetery. We then bear right and take the concrete track up the eastern side of the cemetery to join a broad path climbing steadily to a major junction (**Wp.2 10M**), where we bear right again. One hundred metres later we leave the slightly better trodden goat-tracks and bear left, crossing two terraces and climbing steadily through the oak forest to a rough bridge over the broad **Acequia de Busquístar** (**Wp.3, 15M**).

The path continues climbing steadily before gradually levelling off for an agreeable stroll through the oak forest. After crossing the **Barranco del Tesoro** and its affluents (**Wp.4, 35M**) it climbs to join a dirt track (**Wp.5, 40M**) for a slightly tedious climb round the **Barranco de los Alacranes**. Ignoring branches to the right at 30 metres, 10 minutes and 20 minutes from **Wp.5**, we climb steadily through mixed oak and chestnut. Just after the third branch on the right, the track ends among beehives (the **Cristina Mine**). Here we take the narrow wayposted path on the right (**Wp.6, 60M**) and bear right when it joins another path two minutes later.

This path winds around the head of the **Barrancos de los Alacranes** and **del Pajonal**, dipping up and down through the main channels and innumerable affluents (all dry), before emerging from the oak forest onto an open area of scrubland running up to a junction of paths above a large, recently built reservoir (**Wp.7, 80M**).

We maintain direction along the wayposted branch to skirt behind a pine forest before descending into the **Barranco de los Alisos (Wp.8, 90M)** distinguished by its breadth and several silt-catching dykes. After a brief but stiff climb out of the *barranco*, the path gradually levels off and continues skirting the top of the pine forest before crossing the **Barranco de los Sanos**, after which another level stretch amidst pine and oak leads up to a rocky outcrop just in front of the **Cortijo de la Roza de Garcia (Wp.9, 110M)**.

Ignoring the main path descending to the right of a stand of pine, we take the minor path above the pine maintaining a northerly direction until, shortly after it dips into a stand of oak, the path joins a broad dirt track (Pista Forestal 4, **Wp.10, 125M**). We then follow the dirt track round the head of a major affluent until the track widens and bears left towards the head of the **Bina**, where a narrow GR-waymarked path on the right (**Wp.11, 135M**) descends very steeply down the spit of land dividing the affluent from the main *barranco*. The path zigzags down through pine and oak before bearing left to cross an *acequia* for a final steep descent to the welcome oasis of the **Bina (Wp.12, 150M)** the only *barranco* on this route likely to have any water in it.

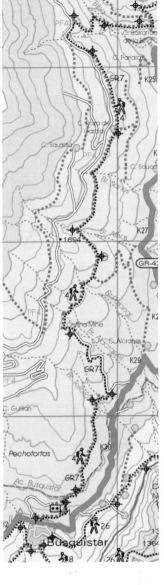

The path out of the *barranco* climbs steeply (E) along the left bank of the **Bina** (thankfully not so steeply as on the right bank) to a rough wire and wood gate. We bear right shortly after this gate for a gentle descent to another gate, after which the path winds along the hillside to pass behind a white-painted ruin with deeply fissured walls (**Cortijo Barranco de la Bina Wp.13, 165M**), where it resumes climbing steeply, passing a series of wayposts and occasional waymarks and cairns, before bearing left towards the head of the *barranco.*

We take the third turning on the right (**Wp.14, 180M** marked by three wayposts) into the pine wood and, after a brief level section, resume the inevitable criss-crossing of subsidiary *barrancos*, fortunately much shallower here. After the fourth dry watercourse, we

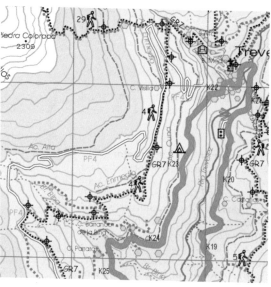

ignore a branch on the right and follow the main traces on the left, emerging from the pine 150 metres later to climb along an exposed ridge.

Ignoring a minor branch to the left, we cross a barbed-wire fence/gate to climb gently through scattered rocks and pine, passing below a ruined *cortijo*, after which we see **Trevélez** clearly. Maintaining direction, we then wind round the mountainside to eventually rejoin Pista Forestal 4 (**Wp.15, 205M**).

(NB If you're coming from **Trevélez**, this turning is not well indicated. It comes 600 metres after you join the Pista Forestal near a grassy platform with a waypost and an apple tree. The clear narrow path is on the left, a few metres before a line of pine and is marked on your right by a small GR cross on a rock in the embankment.)

For **Trevélez**, we follow the dirt track north (**N**) for 600 metres and then bear right onto a narrow blackberry-lined path (**Wp.16, 215M**) which descends to re-cross the dirt track lower down (**Wp.17, 220M**). We continue along this path, crossing the **Río Chico** and following the left bank of the river into **Trevélez' Barrio Alto** at the end of **Calle Charquillo (Wp.18, 225M)**, a considerably more attractive arrival in the town than that endured by those hapless souls dragging round the mountains in their cars and coaches, fetching up in the dreary tourist strip down by the river. Sadly though, that's where we've got to go if we want to catch the bus back to **Busquístar**!

(N.B. If you're doing this route in reverse, ignore a branch on the right between the **Río Chico** and **Wp.17**. This is Wp.14 of Walk 29, the way up to the **Mirador de Trevélez**.)

5. GR7:
TREVÉLEZ - JUVILES

This section of the GR7 starts with an easy climb through pine and craggy rocks with an agreeably 'high-mountain' feel. The descent to **Juviles** is more exposed and might be a bit hot in the height of summer. The route can easily be done in reverse, since the waymarks out of **Juviles** appear to have been made with an east-west trajectory in mind. Park next to the bridge at the bottom of **Trevélez**.

(one way)

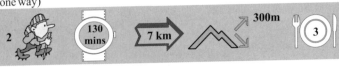

2   130 mins   7 km   300m   3

Buses back   (from **Juviles**) 5.15 p.m.
                    (from **Trevélez**) 3.15 p.m. / 8.30 p.m.

Eighty metres after the **Rio Trevélez** bridge, we take the wayposted path ('Juviles, 3h', **Wp.1, 0M**) climbing **SE**. Ignoring a branch on the left in front of a small spring, we bear right to cross the remains of an abandoned *acequia*. After climbing steadily and passing two houses, we cross a second *acequia*, the **Acequia de Cástaras** (**Wp.2, 10M**) and bear right, ignoring all branch paths, notably the way up to **Peñabón** (an alternative route to the villages of the Eastern Alpujarras, see Walk 30). The GR7 descends slightly to cross the **Calvario** gully then climbs to a small concrete hut (**Wp.3, 25M**) opposite **Trevélez** campsite.

We take the higher of two paths heading south (**S**) from the hut to join a slightly confused and poorly marked section into the **Barranco de los Castaños**. Maintaining level and direction, we aim for the large threshing circle behind the **Cortijo de los Castaños**, 100m before which the path crosses a grassy area fringed with chestnuts (**Wp.4, 35M**) before bearing left just above the chestnuts.

Skirting the southern side of the grassy slope, we head toward an ash at the top of the wood. We then bear right (**S**) at the ash, staying above the wood, before descending onto a lower terrace and a clearer path running up to a ford across the **Castaños** torrent, where there are two unmarked paths.

Ignoring the broader path on the right, we take the narrower path climbing steeply away from the torrent. As the path splinters, we stick to the higher traces, passing two level stretches and the retaining wall of a small reservoir before crossing a meagre affluent stream. The path gradually climbs out of the *barranco* through mixed pine and oak before broadening into a logging track amid more homogenous wood, some 30 minutes from the

Suggested Strolls

From **Trevélez** Wps. 1-3

From **Juviles** climb to **Wp.11** then bear right and follow the dirt track back down to the east of the village.

Cortijo de los Castaños.

We follow the logging track, bearing right as it joins better stabilised tracks (**Wps.5+6, 70M & 80M**) until we reach a crossroads of dirt tracks and firebreaks (**Wp.7, 90M**), where the route becomes more exposed, crossing a scrubland of broom, thyme, gorse and alyssum. We continue straight ahead on a rough track between wire fences and, at the end of the fencing, bear right onto a narrow wayposted path across the scrub (**Wp.8, 92M**) crossing a succession of gullies and small ravines.

Immediately after the second slightly deeper gully, a waypost indicates that the GR7 leaves the main traces and bears right (**Wp.9, 100M**) before resuming a **SE** direction towards **Juviles**, the southernmost houses of which are now visible. The same bearings hold after crossing another gully, this one distinguished by a small grassy patch with an eglantine bush in the middle: bear right alongside the gully, then left towards **Juviles**. After crossing several minor gullies, the path leads onto a spur from where **Juviles** is clearly visible – happily, as the waymarks have all been painted for people coming in the opposite direction.

The path broadens as it descends this spur before bearing left to cross a dirt track (**Wp.10, 115M**), beyond which we can either follow a minor branch track or take the poorly wayposted shortcuts down to a couple of white water huts above a reservoir. Passing to the left of the reservoir, we cross a broad bare slope to twin waymarked holm oaks, below which there is a rough dirt track (**Wp.11, 125M**). We turn right and, 10 metres later, leave the dirt track to take a narrow unmarked path between fields and orchards, joining a broad concrete lane next to a water hut which leads into the centre of **Juviles** (**Wp.12, 130M**).

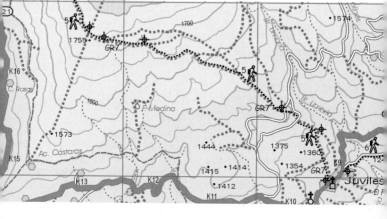

6. GR7:

JUVILES - CÁDIAR
+ extension between CÁDIAR & LOBRAS

An attractive, low mountain walk of contrasts, linking some wild, secluded spots with areas of thoroughly domesticated landscape, and several of the Alpujarras' less celebrated settlements. **Tímar** and **Lobras** in particular are sleepy little hamlets that seem wholly unaware of the tourists trundling through the more famous villages to the north. I don't recommend this route in the height of summer, but it's ideal for winter, or spring and autumn evenings. The extension gives the option of making loop between **Lobras** and **Cádiar** via the GR142. There's also a link with the GR142 back to **Busquístar** for longer circuits (see Walk 8). There's plenty of parking along the main road through **Juviles**.

Timing
Juviles-Cádiar 2 hours 40 mins (one-way)
Cádiar-Lobras 1 hour 50 mins (one-way)
Lobras-Cádiar loop 3 hours

NB
Beware of the official waypost times; if they are to be believed, the **Juviles-Tímar** stretch takes 45 minutes downhill and 40 minutes uphill, the GR142 between **Cádiar** and **Lobras** makes no progress whatsoever in the course of twenty minutes' walking, while a 100 metre stroll past the chemist in **Lobras** sets you back half-an-hour!

Estimated Distances:
Juviles-Cádiar 8km, **Cádiar-Lobras** 7km, **Lobras - Cádiar** Loop 10km

Buses back: don't exist, however there is a bus from **Cádiar** to **Órgiva** (5 p.m.) where you could pick up the 6.45 p.m. bus to **Juviles**; alternatively, if you're feeling energetic, in a little over an hour you can climb to **Alcútar** (see Walk 7) for the 5 p.m. bus to **Juviles**.

From the eastern limit of **Juviles**, next to the Jamones de Juviles building (**Wp.1, 0M**), we take the **Calle Escuela** and bear left after 50m onto a waypost dirt track. We then follow the dirt track across the **Barranco de Umbría**, ignoring a branch on the left as we climb towards **El Fuerte**, the rocky outcrop separating **Juviles** from **Tímar**.

The track dwindles to a path that crosses an *acequia* shortly before a junction (**Wp.2, 15M**). The branch on the right climbs **El Fuerte**, but we bear left, staying on the GR7 down to the dramatic pass at the head of the **Barranco de Lobras** between **El Fuerte** and the **Alto del Calar**, where there's another

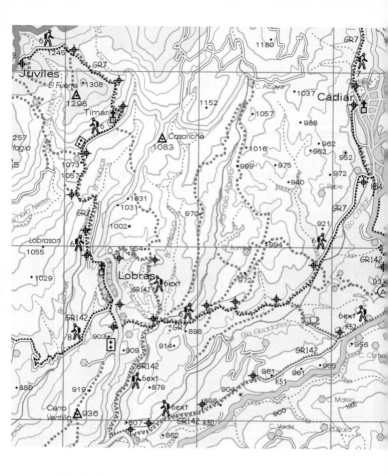

waypost (**Wp.3, 25M**) and a clear rocky path down to the north-eastern tip of **Tímar** (**Wp.4, 35M**).

After descending to **Tímar** church, we bear right along the concrete lane fronting the village to join a dirt track which we follow (contrary to what other maps tell you) all the way to the cemetery. The track descends past the cemetery to an unusual threshing circle (**Wp.5, 45M**) pebbled like a sundial, after which it dwindles to a mule trail through orchards and olive groves.

Ignoring two cobbled branches to the left, we stay on the main trail till it leaves the cultivated terraces to cross scrubland and a rough firebreak before descending to a badly eroded col with a dirt track running in from the right (**NW, Wp.6, 55M**). We turn left here on a clear path down into the **Barranco de Lobras**.

On the far side of the *barranco*, the path climbs **SSE**, gently at first then more steeply, before levelling out alongside a concrete *acequia* (**Wp.7, 70M**). We bear right along the *acequia* path until a junction of dirt tracks (**Wp.8, 72M**) where we turn left on the main track and, after 50m, join the road just north of

Lobras (Wayposted 'Tímar 40').

For refreshment, there's a pokey but pleasing little bar off the square behind the church, otherwise we stay on the main road past the village (**S**), passing the GR142 (**E**) to **Cádiar** (on the left after the *fuente*). We then 'lose' 30' (watch the wayposts) and pass the GR142 (**W**) to **Busquístar**, soon after which we turn left on a narrow path between a parking area and a building with red doors and a vine arbour (**Wp.9, 90M**).

<table>
<tr><td>

Suggested Strolls

Juviles – El Fuerte (turn right at **Wp.2**)

Juviles – Tímar (**Wps. 1-4**)

Tímar – Lobras (**Wps. 5**-8) returning via the road

Lobras – Junta de los Barrancos via the GRs (**Wps. 9/10/25/26**)

Cádiar – Río Guadalfeo (Wps. 16-13)

Rambla Vereda From the A-348 take the **Lobras** road down to the **Río Guadalfeo** and park at the bridge. Stroll along the *barranco* to the junction of the GRs (**Wps. 24 & 10**).

</td><td>

The narrow path leads to an almond grove and a mule trail winding down between olive groves to the junction of the **Barrancos de Escalona & Atalaya** where the GRs 7 & 142 intersect again (**Wp.10, 100M**). Beyond the GR junction, we cross the *rambla* into an abandoned olive grove where a broad goat track climbs steeply on the right. Ignoring the goat track, we bear left, heading for a clearly waymarked stump, beyond which a waypost marks the start of a path that climbs less abruptly.

The GR7 follows this well-marked path as it winds up a *retama* covered hillside to a fig orchard (NB windfalls have seeded themselves along the path and give great fruit in early autumn, unlike most wild figs which normally dry and rot without ripening) where it crosses a dirt track (**Wp.11, 110M**) before continuing through scrub and levelling out above the tree-lined **Río Guadalfeo**.

After winding round the head of a small gully, a gradual descent leads to an *acequia* where, after a very brief climb towards a scattering of olive trees, we bear right at a junction (**Wp.12, 120M**) to cross the *acequia*. We then follow the *acequia* till the path dips down at a fine blackberry bush (another reason for doing this route in autumn), after which it re-crosses the *acequia* and runs along a carefully built retaining wall to pass a ruin and an unmarked junction of dirt tracks (**Wp.13, 125M**).

</td></tr>
</table>

We carry straight on, passing another junction a couple of minutes later with a signposted path on the right – 'Alqueria de Moraya Hotel/Restaurant 500m' (see Appendix C). NB If you're doing the circuit and want to avoid the section of the G142 on the road, you could take this path to **Wp.19**.

Otherwise, continue on the main dirt track, bearing left as it feeds into another dirt track (**Wp.14, 135M**) which leads to a footbridge/ford/abandoned road bridge (**Wp.15 150M**) just to the south of **Cádiar**.

If you want to do the full loop
If you want to do the full loop, cross the river here and climb to the main road.

To go into Cádiar centre
If you want to go into the centre of **Cádiar**, continue along the right bank of what is now the **Río Cádiar**, crossing the river just before a small concrete bridge with green railings, shortly after which you'll find a GR7 signpost saying 'Lobras 1h45' (**Wp.16, 160M**) NW of the church and the municipal market.

Suggested Strolls

Heading east off the map, the GR142 **Venta de Cuatro Caminos** to **Cortijo Fuente La Virgen**. From the disused concrete bridge at the southern end of **Cádiar (Wp.15)**, take the slip road 300 metres up to turn right on the A348 by-pass, setting the odometer at 0 at the junction with the main road. At 700 metres, turn left on a dirt track to join the GR142 (**Wp.16** EXT* /**Cuatro Caminos**) on a loop of the old road. Follow the dirt track, the **Rambla de Retenil**, to the **Fuente de la Virgen** *cortijo* at the end of the dramatic cliffs just past an abandoned factory.

NB This route can also be done by car in dry conditions. The GR142 continues (off our map) to **Jorairátar**.

EXTENSION:
For the GR142 from **Cádiar** to **Lobras**, from **Wp.15** we follow the **Venta de Cuatro Caminos** stroll (on foot, alas, and without the odometer - see above) to (**Wp.16** EXT*) then head west rather than east, following the *rambla* through the tunnel under the road and, 100 metres later, bearing left to climb over a rise to a wayposted dirt track (**Wp.17, 10M** from **Wp.15**). After bearing left then left again at an unmarked junction (**Wp.18, 15M**), we rejoin the A-348 (this is the GR142 after all!). We then follow the road to the junction with the A-345 and turn right to continue along the A-348 to the driveway of the **Alqueria de Moraya Hotel (Wp.19, 25M)**.

From the driveway, we take the dirt track climbing the ridge on the left for fine views of the **Sierra Nevada**. Ignoring a branch on the left, we follow the dirt track till it bears right. We leave the dirt track next to a waypost and two waymarked trees (**Wp.20, 40M**) and descend to the left of an old reservoir alongside a newly planted vineyard. The path may be ploughed up after the reservoir, in which case we maintain a south-west to westerly direction toward a small ruin, just before which there are a couple of wayposts.

Leaving the ruin on our right, we take a rough dirt track across an almond grove, crossing another track (**Wp.21, 50M**) to continue (**SWW**) through a field of almonds and figs. When the dirt track along the ridge eventually peters out, we bear right and follow a firebreak until it dips down to a small col (**Wp.22, 60M**). Taking the broad path on the right, we descend rapidly to rejoin the firebreak, which we follow down a steep slope to a ruined mill at the junction of the **Río Guadalfeo** and the **Barranco del Lagarto** (**Wp.23, 65M**).

We then cross the **Guadalfeo** and, 100m after the bridge, bear right (**Wp.24, 70M**) into the **Rambla Vereda** running up to the **Barrancos de Escalona & Atalaya**. After ten minutes a GR-sign 'Lobras 1h' seems to send us up a hill on the right, but in fact the itinerary continues along the riverbed for an attractively wild stroll to the junction of the GRs (**Wp.10**) twenty minutes from the road.

The GR142 climbs the spur to the north between the two *barrancos*, though you wouldn't know it from the waymarks. Ignoring the clearer goat tracks to the left of the ridge, we bear right from the tip of the spur and scramble straight up the ridge for a steep climb to a waymarked concrete electricity pylon.

Behind the pylon, a firebreak runs up to a waypost (**Wp.25, 100M**) where the GR leaves the firebreak and bears left to cross two gullies before climbing to a threshing circle next to an acacia tree. Bearing right (**N**) away from the threshing circle, we skirt the head of another gully and follow the goat tracks into **Lobras** (**Wp.26, 120M**).

CÁDIAR - BÉRCHULES
MECINA-BOMBARÓN

A 'commuting path' linking the three villages at the eastern limit of our map. The landscape is relatively domestic, but no less interesting for that, and the villages are just as attractive as the better known ones to the west, perhaps even more so since they are free of the more garish symptoms of tourism. **Bérchules**, in particular, is an unjustly neglected village with full services and some great walks. There are plenty of bars and restaurants en route and, with an early start, this walk could lead to a leisurely lunch in **Mecina-Bombarón** before taking the afternoon bus back to **Cádiar**.

(one way)

3   3 hours   9 km   550m   5

Buses back: 4.30 p.m.

Parking in the **Plaza de la Iglesia** in **Cádiar** (**Wp.1, 0M**), we take the street behind the *Mercado Municipal*, then the concrete lane down to the **Río Cádiar**. Bearing right at the GR7 waypost ('Lobras 1h45' / Walk 6), we follow the partially concreted track between orchards and houses. When the track turns left toward the river (**Wp.2, 10M**), we bear right along a path between fields, rejoining the dirt track five minutes later. The track soon runs into the dry riverbed where it dwindles to a path.

After climbing back onto the embankment to bypass a large pipe across the river, the traces become rather confused. Ignoring the apparently clearer route on the right bank beside the poplars, we stay on or near the left bank until we're level with **Narila** church-tower, where a clear but confusingly waymarked path leads away from the river to cross a small *acequia* and climb into **Narila** just below a well-maintained house with a millstone propped beside its front door (**Wp.3, 25M**).

To cross **Narila**, we take the first concreted lane on the left, then first left again. We then follow this street until it bears right past a walled garden with a fig tree at one end and a walnut at the other, then turn left at the T-junction and follow the concrete lane to the northern end of the village, where a GR7 waypost beside a large water hut indicates 'Alcútar 1h' (**Wp.4, 30M**).

We follow the concrete lane back down to the river, ignoring a track and a path climbing to the right and, shortly after the concrete gives way to dirt, a

Suggested Strolls
Cádiar – Narila (**Wps. 1-3**)
Bérchules Camino al Río (**Wps. 8-9**). Bear right just before **Wp.9** for a fine bathing pool 100 metres down river (but beware of slippery rocks).

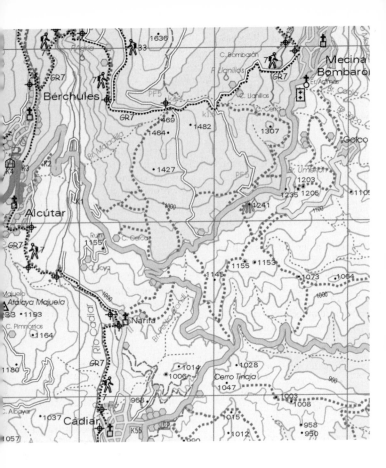

branch on the left into the riverbed. Staying on the main dirt track for a gentle climb past a stand of poplars, we bear left (just before another concreted section) on a rough dirt track across the river, where another narrow dirt track climbs to a Y-junction.

Bearing right at the Y-junction, we follow the dirt track for an increasingly steep climb to a terrace, where the GR7 turns right onto a broad path (**Wp.5, 45M**) that soon turns into a rock-laid mule trail. We then follow the mule trail as it winds up between the terraces to cross another dirt track (**Wp.6, 55M**) before coming into the lower part of **Alcútar** behind a large farm building (**Wp.7, 70M**).

Bearing left on a partially concreted lane, we climb steeply into the village to pass a GR7 waypost, 'Narila 40''. We then turn right at the junction just after the waypost and follow the alley as it bears left after House No. 6, then right along the **Calle Cantera** into the **Plaza de la Iglesia**. Beyond this *plaza* are the supermarket and the main road (gr-421) which we take, at some peril to life and limb, up to **Bérchules**.

Following the road into **Bérchules**, we pass a miraculous *fuente* which might come in handy if you're feeling lonely, since one drink of its waters is supposed to guarantee the instant attainment of an ideal spouse. Spouse or no, our itinerary then takes the **Calle Iglesia** past the church, crosses the **Plaza Abastos**, and follows the **Calle Real** before bearing right on the **Calle Agua**, at the end of which (**Wp.8, 95M**) you'll find the **Camino al Río** and the GR7 waypost, 'Mecina-Bombarón 2h'.

The path descends rapidly, crossing a litter strewn watercourse, after which it levels out for a couple of minutes before starting its final descent from a threshing circle down to the bridge over the **Río Grande** (**Wp.9, 110M**). On the far side of the river, a rock-laid path (where one can occasionally see *cabra montés*) zigzags up a gully before bearing right on a dirt stretch leading to an old stone wall.

We climb alongside this wall and, when it ends, continue climbing (**SE**) until the path broadens briefly before running into a junction (**Wp.10, 135M**). Taking the wayposted branch on the right, we pass a few almond trees before bearing right towards a small stone byre. Passing in front of the byre, we follow a stone terracing wall, after which a gentle climb along a clear path (**S**) leads to a dirt track (**Wp.11, 145M**).

We bear right here for a brief climb before the track levels off and joins another larger dirt track (**Wp.12, 155M** / PF5) which we follow (**E**) all the way to **Mecina-Bombarón**. Shortly after a concreted stretch through pine trees, we ignore a major branch on the right and bear left towards a large water reservoir and the **Mecina** satellite communications tower. We also ignore a major branch off to the left a little way above the communications tower. 200m after the tower, the track, now concreted, arrives in **Mecina-Bombarón's Plaza Vieja** (**Wp.13, 180M**).

Suggested Strolls

The section of the GR7 covered by our map does not actually end here and you may wish to extend your walk to **Golco** or try one of the following strolls (NB the bus does not stop at **Golco**).

Mecina-Bombarón – Golco
From the central square on the main road through **Mecina-Bombarón**, take the **Calle Iglesia Vieja** below the GR7 waypost, 'Golco 20''. Bear right after a second waypost onto a concreted lane which runs into two dirt paths. Take the broad path on the right to arrive in **Golco** a few metres above the **Golco Camino al Río**.

Golco Camino al Río
30m behind the church, take the concrete lane down past the lower part of the village, passing a little picnic spot, where the concrete turns to dirt. Shortly after a second narrow concreted section, just as the track bears right, turn left onto a narrow path down to a large threshing circle, after which a rough path descends to a another narrow dirt track. Bear left then right at the Y-junction, where the track dwindles to a path descending to the river and a pleasant picnic spot, beyond which the GR7 continues to **Montenegro** and **Yegen**.

8. GR142:
LOBRAS - BUSQUÍSTAR

Dipping up and down like a roller coaster, this stretch of the GR142 can seem quite gruelling, but though it boasts some classic GR142 qualities (see Introduction), it also appeals to more conventional ramblers' criteria. The mule trails adjacent to **Notáez** are as nice as any in the **Tahá**, **Cástaras** is a lovely little oasis of green, and the route also provides a useful link between sections of the GR7. If you haven't yet done any walks in the **Tahá**, this will also be your first introduction to the remarkable passes through the **Sierra Mecina** (**Wp.11+**) that were so vital to the Moorish silk trade. It's a relatively complicated itinerary, but surprisingly well waymarked, and nobody has, as yet, concluded it would be a witty idea to uproot the waypoints. Best in the cooler seasons, but pleasant in the summer if you start early in the morning or late in the afternoon. It could easily be done in the opposite direction, taking the '**Camino del Río**' from **Busquístar** then following the GR waymarks.

(one way)

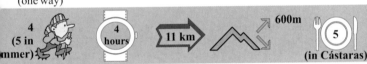

| 4 (5 in summer) | 4 hours | 11 km | ⌃⌄ 600m | 5 (in Cástaras) |

Buses back: no direct buses, though if you set off early, you could catch the 2.55 p.m. to **Juviles** and follow Walk 6 back to **Lobras**. Beware of doing it both ways on a summer's day; I did it and it was not a good idea.

To reach the start, we take the concrete alley out of **Lobras** church square, to the right of the *correos* office. We then bear left at the Y-junction just beyond a small *fuente* and follow the main road down to a GR signpost, 'Cádiar 1h45 / Nieles 1h30' (**Wp.1, 0M**).

Here we bear right on the concrete (later dirt) track down to the **Barranco de Lobras**, beyond which the track winds up the Lobrasan rise and bears left above the **Barranco de la Cabaña**. One hundred metres after a couple of electricity pylons (one metal, one concrete) we leave the dirt track (**Wp.2, 35M**) and turn right to skirt an almond grove with a large waymarked olive tree on our left.

At the top of the almond grove, we bear left onto a rough farm track climbing past a breeze-block hut, after which it becomes increasingly overgrown. One hundred metres after a shallow cutting and two large *acequia* taps, the track bears right in sight of **Nieles** and we take the narrow path on the left (**Wp.3, 45M**) gradually descending into the **Rambla de Nieles**.

After crossing the shallow stream (**Wp.4, 55M**) at the bottom of the valley, we climb a rough path on the other side that soon runs into an ancient mule trail. The trail crosses an eroded stretch after about ten minutes and enters **Nieles** above a *lavadero* (**Wp.5, 70M**), where we turn left onto the road signposted for **Cástaras**.

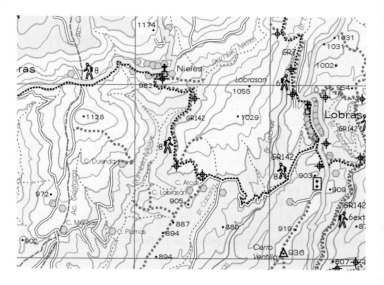

The road climbs to pass under an aqueduct from where you can see the tip of **Cástaras** perched on the cliffs overlooking the **Rambla de Cástaras**. Glance left and right, and you will appreciate why the GR follows the road here, all options involving a very rough climb or a very rough descent. Entering **Cástaras**, we go to the right of the church (**Wp.6, 100M**) passing (on our right, and definitely worth visiting) the last bar before **Busquístar**. We then take the street in front of the church doors up to a four-spouted fountain and the **Bar/Pension Maria** (usually closed, but apparently you only have to knock to find a bed for the night).

The alley on the right immediately beyond the bar leads us to a waymarked stone pillar, from where a concrete track descends to an *acequia*, the gated entrance to a house and, on the right, the GR142 path. This path crosses the **Barrancos de Fuente Medina** and **Alberquilla** to join a mule trail leading towards the cemetery. When the main trail bears left in a **SE** direction toward the cemetery, we take the rougher trail (**Wp.7, 115M**) climbing to the right. We then cross the new dirt track to the cemetery and follow the path as it climbs towards the **Cástaras-Torviscón** road.

The path levels out for 10-15 minutes, passing between almond groves till it gradually descends and actually runs into an almond grove at a point marked by three wayposts (**Wp.8, 135M**). Bearing right, we cross the middle of the almond grove, coming into sight of **Notáez** about halfway across. Toward the edge of the almond grove, the GR bears left past a couple of waymarked trees, at the second of which it turns sharp left onto a narrow path zigzagging down the slope to come out behind the rocky spine to the **SW**.

> **Suggested Strolls**
>
> From the junction of the **Trevélez/Cástaras** roads (**Wp.11**), take the GR142 until the steep descent begins at the rock-laid section.
>
> Start of **Notáez – Cástaras (Wps. 9-8)**
>
> Start of **Cástaras – Notáez (Wps. 6-7)**; bear left when the mule trail crosses the cemetery track which we follow onto the promontory.

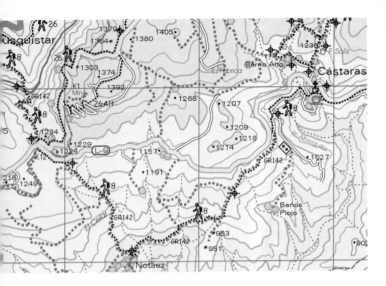

Ignoring the tractor tracks that descend all the way to the spine, we follow the narrow path as it bears right, away from the spine, towards **Notáez**. After crossing a small dry *barranco* and descending through yet another almond grove, the path follows the contour lines to join a partially rock-laid mule trail.

After a broad, sandy stretch, the mule trail makes a final zigzagging descent to cross a bridge over one of the affluents of the **Rambla de Notáez**, then climbs into the village beside two GR waypoints (**Wp.9, 150M**) indicating 'Cástaras 1h30 / Busquístar 2h', where we immediately climb to the right (Yes, I know!).

The pitted concrete track out of **Notáez** soon gives way to a dirt path climbing past allotments and olive and almond terraces, eventually emerging onto scrubland below the daunting cliffs of **El Celar**. Beyond **El Celar**, we cross an almond grove (possibly ploughed) and immediately bear left onto a narrow path over an embrambled *rambla*.

Suggested Strolls

Busquístar, Camino al Río. From the main square in **Busquístar**, take the concrete lane to the right of the Bar Vargas. Bear right, away from the 'Camino Helechal' (Walk 26), then take the second left and follow the concrete lane down to the **Camino al Río** sign (**Wp.13**) and the path down to the river. Just before the bridge (**Wp.12**), a path on he left goes upriver past several plunge-pools to the old electricity installations.

We then skirt a field of fig saplings and climb through a wilderness of *retama* (this is the GR142!) before passing under some power lines and crossing an *acequia* to join the road from **Cástaras** (**Wp.10, 195M**). Obviously, if you don't want to descend 200-odd metres just to climb again, this road is an alternative route. Equally obviously, it's a lot less attractive.

Bearing left, we follow the road to the **Trevélez** junction, from where we can see **Busquístar**, which a waypost (**Wp.11, 200M**) claims is one hour away. We leave the road, ignoring the path into the gully and follow the higher path which crosses a slope then descends below the old iron mines of **Cerro del Conjuro**.

After swinging left to cross the gully, the path comes to a rock shelf and begins its extremely dramatic descent into the gorge, following a broad, rocky route down to a bridge over the **Rio Trevélez (Wp.12, 220M)**. NB A slip path just before the bridge leads to a swimmable pool (concealed by trees and a boulder). More private bathing points can be found by following the path on the right bank upriver to the old electricity installations.

From the river, it's a fifteen minute climb to **Busquístar (Wp.13, 240M)** along a clear path arriving at the 'Camino al Río /GR142 Notáez 1h30' signs.

9. GR142:
ÓRGIVA - LANJARÓN

Not the most the most breathtaking of paths (though you may be a bit puffed) and not recommended at the height of the day in summer, but a useful route for long-distance walkers and those wishing to link up with the GR7 (Walk 1) or explore the mountains above **Lanjarón** (Walks 11 & 12). Park just before the BP station at the north-west end of **Órgiva**, where you can usually find a space in the shade.

(one way)

3   2 hours   6 km   400m   5

Buses back: 12 a.m., 1.30 p.m., 5.45 p.m.

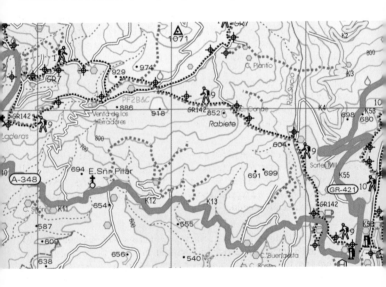

Passing **Órgiva** BP station, we cross the bridge over the **Río Chico** (**Wp.1, 0M**/km16 of the A-348) and turn right on the gr-421, taking the clear path on the left fifty metres later (**Wp.2, 2M**). This unmarked path meanders through terraces of olive, orange, lemon and mulberry trees, and passes behind an abandoned factory before joining a partially concreted track (**Wp.3, 10M**) leading onto the A-348 to **Lanjarón**.

The official route bears right and follows the road for five minutes to the **Río Sucio** bridge just after the **Venta Maria** bar. For a nicer route, I suggest ignoring the GR cross and turning left on the road.

> **Suggested Strolls**
>
> **Río Sucio** (Wps. 5-6)

Then, after fifty metres we turn right down a lane (**Wp.4, 12M**) and bear right almost immediately on a dirt track which dwindles to a path passing between a small house and trellised fig trees. Once past the house, we follow a narrow path along an old *acequia* to the **Río Sucio** bridge (**Wp.5, 15M**), where we cross the road and take the waymarked track up the left bank of the river.

Shortly after a house shrouded in eucalyptus, the track goes between a waypost (uprooted at the time of writing) and a stone corral with a fig tree (**Wp.6, 30M**), where we bear left into the riverbed then climb the bluffs on the far side. The path (at first clearly waymarked) climbs steadily and then steeply up the western side of the valley toward a large outcrop of rock, the **Rabiete** (**Wp.7, 55M**).

Just before the **Rabiete**, we bear right for a gentler climb past more terraces of olive, almond, and fig trees to come out behind a *cortijo* (**Wp.8 65M**), usually mapped as the **Cortijo de Meridas** though better known to locals as the **Cortijo de Conde** or **de Tejas** since the *Conde* in question was the only man wealthy enough to roof his house with tiles. The traditional roofing material here is *launa*, a kind of heavy duty daub mixed from the local mica.

Unless you want to join the GR7 (see Walk 1, Wp.8), stay above the farm track and bear away from the *cortijo* (**W**), following the higher traces amid a maze of goat tracks occasionally waymarked with red and/or very old yellow dots. We continue in this direction staying ten to fifteen metres above a dry watercourse lined with poplars and eucalyptus, following increasingly infrequent and faint yellow dots till a small pond-like reservoir (**Wp.9, 75M**) on our right. After the reservoir, we bear slightly left on the yellow path (**NWW**) until it joins a dirt track (PF1 Branch C) beside a waypost (**Wp.10, 80M**) a few metres below the GR7 (see Walk 1, Wp.7).

We then turn left along the *pista forestal*, which soon reaches a stretch of concrete. Just before the concrete ends, we turn right next to a house with a tall weeping willow, the **Venta de los Herradores** (**Wp.11, 90M**). Taking the path behind the house, we rejoin the *pista forestal*, again concreted, which we follow down to a small aqueduct (**Wp.12, 95M**).

Here we bear left and follow a dirt track until it crosses an *acequia* (**Wp.13, 110M**) behind a small *ermita* overlooking Lanjarón. On the western side of the *acequia*, we turn right onto a narrow path and zigzag down to rejoin the *pista forestal* into **Lanjarón**, arriving at the road (**Wp.14, 120M**), a few metres from the start of the GR7 to **Cáñar**. We then follow the A-348 into **Lanjarón** where there are plenty of bars, restaurants and hotels. The spa is situated at the western end of town.

10. JEANNETTE'S ACEQUIA WALK: BAYACAS - ÓRGIVA - BAYACAS

So-called because it was discovered by Jeannette while the author was having a nap in the front seat of the car. An attractive, strikingly varied circuit, including an easy climb up the ridge between the **Ríos Seco** and **Chico**, a tour through **Órgiva**, a breathtaking scramble, and a lovely green tunnel alongside a little known *acequia*. The last part in particular is remarkable: a stroll that seems like an adventure! Parking in **Bayacas** is no problem. If you start from **Órgiva**, park as per Walk 9.

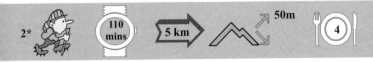

2*	110 mins	5 km	⛰️	50m	🍴 4

* (except for one very short section between **Wps. 7 & 8** which is 4)

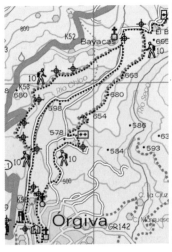

Starting from the schoolhouse behind **Bayacas** church tower (**Wp.1, 0M**), we cross the bridge over the **Río Chico**, then turn left and follow the dirt track upriver for 100 metres. We then turn right onto another track passing a two-storey concrete house, behind which the track dwindles to a path leading to a tiny concrete bridge (**Wp.2, 6M**) over an *acequia*. Ignoring the waymarked track up to **El Barrio**, we turn right on the *acequia* path.

We then bear left shortly after a ruin and go behind a small white-walled cabin to continue along the *acequia* (**S**), ignoring a turning to the right after a byre. When the main path descends left toward a white-walled cabin, just after some pomegranate and quince trees, we bear right for a gentle climb to the goat tracks along the ridge.

Follow the clearer tracks to the left of the first rocky outcrop until you can see where the ridge dips down to a col leading into a clear path south. As the clearer goat tracks veer away to the left, we bear right (**SSW**) along fainter tracks up to the col where the escarpment drops dramatically to the **Río Chico**. The path continues along the ridge, coming into view of **Órgiva** through a stretch of pine and, as it crosses open scrubland, the cemetery.

When the path joins a dirt track climbing from the **Río Chico**, we turn left to pass the cemetery and descend to a huge green telecommunications mast, where we leave the main track, bearing left on a rougher track then right at the junction with a broader track (**Wp.3, 40M**).

This broad track soon turns into a tarmac road that swings left after an aqueduct and comes within sight of the **Ermita de San Sebastian**. The road curves round the garden of a big house with a large swimming pool then bears left past an outhouse with a trellis on the roof. We turn right onto a lane (**Wp.4, 50M**) opposite the outhouse, then left almost immediately on a narrow path between a house and a high retaining wall. This path emerges at the edge of **Órgiva**, behind the *ermita* on a concrete lane, the **Calle Ermita**.

We follow the **Calle Ermita** to the junction with the **Calle Estación** and turn right on the **Calle Nueva**.

At what appears to be the end of the **Calle Nueva** (in fact it continues to the left) you have two choices, A or B.

A

If you don't want to go into town, take the shortcut path (**Wp.5, 55M**) that descends to the **Río Chico** (**Wp.6, 2M** away) from the right of the long low house in front of you.

B

If you want to go into **Órgiva**, turn left at the 'end' of the **Calle Nueva** and then, after the telephone booth, right on the **Calle Barrio Alto** (identifiable by the **Peluqueria Enriqueta** shop-sign). At the **Panaderia Herredo**, turn left for the high street shops and bars, or right to continue the walk. After the **Fruteria Deron**, bear left and descend to turn right on the main road out of **Órgiva** (**W**).

At the BP station (the starting point if you set off from **Órgiva**), take the tarmac lane leading up to the **Funereria/Carpinteria** and continue between the **Carpinteria** and the **Taller Jorge**, passing various warehouses and workshops which gradually give way to houses. 5m after the house called **El Olivo**, the shortcut path joins this lane (**Wp.6**).

Suggested Strolls	Continuing up the lane, we take the first turning on the left (**Wp.7, 75M** N.B. You could carry on upriver to **Bayacas** but it would be a shame since, though you would miss the most strenuous part of the walk, you'd also miss the prettiest and most exceptional part) crossing the river on a concrete bridge beyond which there's a stand of eucalyptus with some large boulders in front of them.
Bayacas - El Barrio (Wps. 1-2)	
Bayacas Acequia. Setting the odometer at 0 at the start of the road, follow the gr-421 for 1.8 km, then turn right on a dirt track and park in the clearing above the reservoir; follow the *acequia* to **Bayacas** (Wps. 9-12 + 1)	We then follow the track as it bears right and, after 150 metres, turn left onto another more overgrown track. Where this track bears left after 15 metres (**Wp.8, 80M**) there's a slightly bare area on the right which, believe it or not, is the start of the path up!

This is a very rough path up to a point about 30 metres behind the large umbrella pine visible on the ridge above, but it's easy to follow and, though steep, takes less than ten minutes. After a fierce climb, another path comes in from the right next to a small olive tree and a small almond tree. We turn left on this path (a clear view of the pine indicates the ascent is almost over) and continue till we come out behind the pine (largely obscured from here) in a well maintained olive grove lined with quince, bamboo and *retama*. Turning right along the path skirting the olive grove, we soon come to a small clearing (**Wp.9, 90M**), just below the gr-421.

We bear right below the clearing and follow the narrow path along the *acequia*. This is a magical little path, burrowing behind a wall of bamboo into a soothing green tunnel freshened by the tumbling waters of the *acequia*. Unfortunately, if the water has been diverted higher up, the path loses a lot of its charm.

When the path appears to enter a private garden (**Wp.10, 95M**), we continue for a couple of metres and bear round a small willow tree to pass behind the garden, after which the path gets narrower, the bamboo more invasive, as it leads up to a short stretch along a narrow concrete and breeze-block wall.

Just after a large bank of oleander, the path crosses a watercourse, beyond which rough steps (**Wp.11, 97M**) have been cut in the earth climbing towards a wall of bamboo. Ten metres after the steps the *acequia* finally becomes too overgrown to follow unless you fancy crawling. Happily, five metres after the steps there's a gap in the brambles and *retama* on the left, where we can scramble onto a path along a terrace above the *acequia*.

The path may occasionally be overgrown, but pushing on (**NEE**), ignoring alternative descents to the *acequia* and ducking under the branches of an olive tree (watch out for erosion clefts in the path here), we emerge on a well-maintained olive terrace (**Wp.12, 102M**).

Crossing this terrace, we pick up a clear path between immaculately tended orchards of olive, orange and lemon trees and fields of legumes, maize and wheat. In summer you can also see neatly sheaved hand-mown hay. The path soon passes below the white-painted walls of the **Molino de Pancho** before joining the road into **Bayacas** in sight of the church tower (**110M**).

11. CAMINO DE LA SIERRA: LANJARÓN - PUENTE EL VADILLO & CASA FORESTAL DE TELLO

Following a traditional if narrow mule trail, this is an easy well-marked route (red dots) up the left bank of the **Río Lanjarón**, ending at an idyllic picnic spot. The beginning's a bit barren because of forest fires, but the later stretches are blessed with some extraordinarily venerable chestnut trees giving welcome shade in the summer. Water may be available behind the cabin at **Wp.6**. Parking as per Walk 1.

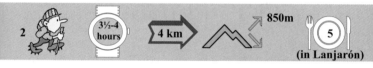

2   3½-4 hours   4 km   850m   5 (in Lanjarón)

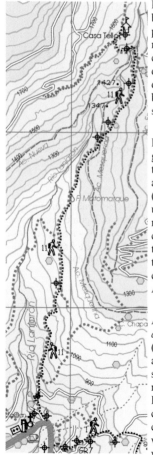

From the eastern end of the **Río Lanjarón** bridge (**Wp.1, 0M**), we take the dirt track (**N**) past the **Fuente Hoya del Grillo** and bear right after seventy-five metres on a partially cobbled path (**Wp.2**) climbing steeply to a dirt track (**Wp.3, 10M**). We then follow the dirt track (**N**) for fifty metres and, when it bears right, continue straight ahead on the stony path/mule trail.

Ignoring all branches we climb steadily, gradually edging away from the river through arid terraces of fire-scorched olive and chestnut till the path joins a dirt track (**Wp.4, 60M**) above the fire-line. We take the upper branch of the track, which soon narrows to a path behind a *cortijo*, then climbs more gently among shady chestnut trees. After crossing three shallow streams, the path climbs steeply between the embankments of two fields and crosses the **Acequia Mezquinera (Wp.5, 90M)**.

After another steep climb beyond the *acequia,* we go to the left of a stone cabin (**Wp.6, 100M**) and continue climbing along a broad unmarked path from where a tall sequoia can be seen on the right bank of the river, marking the as yet invisible **Casa Forestal de Tello**. Ten minutes after the cabin, the path passes above a waterfall and enters another shady stand of chestnuts where a waypost, just below a small cabin with a solar panel, indicates **Tello** on the left

(**Wp.7, 115M**).

Taking the narrow path on the left round the back of an abandoned byre, we pass between two recently renovated cabins, climbing steadily until just after a massive slab of rock on our left, we see the **Vadillo Bridge** down below. Five metres after the rock we turn left on another path and descend to the bridge (**Wp.8, 120M**).

Shortly before the bridge there's a beautiful picnic spot - a grassy oak-shaded platform in front of a waterfall. If you want to continue up to **Tello**, take the steep path after the bridge, crossing the **Acequia Nueva** and a small glade, beyond which is the *casa forestal* (**Wp.9, 130M**). Unless you fancy hair-raising escapades along the **Acequia Nueva** or monotonous descents down dirt tracks, return by the same route (**90M**).

Suggested Strolls

Tello from above. Follow *Pista Forestal* 1 to km 13.2. Turn right, then right again 900 metres later at the Y-junction and park at the end of the **Tello** track. Follow the path down to the *casa forestal*.

---

12. EL CABALLO

If you only have time for one 3000 metre peak, this is the one to do. It's wilder than the **Mulhacén**, less tiring, more interesting, and quite as 'unique', being the westernmost 3000 metre peak of the chain. However, pathfinding may be a problem in winter and there are frequently strong winds in the summer. The terrain is rough, so don't attempt it in poor conditions. Access via **Pista Forestal 1**. Park in the turning circle at the end of the *pista forestal*.

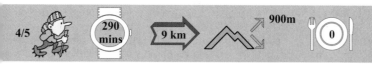

4/5   290 mins   9 km   900m   0

From the end of **PF1 (Wp.1, 0M)**, we take the broad wayposted path climbing **NW**. Ignoring a rough dirt track to the right 50 metres later, we stick to the main path climbing to the partially abandoned but still serviceable **Refugio de Ventura (Wp.2, 20M)**, from where the **Cerro de Caballo** is clearly visible.

One hundred and fifty metres after the refuge, we leave the main path just before a stand of stubby pine, and bear left at a cairn onto a fainter, rougher path climbing steeply towards the ridge. The path soon crosses an *acequia* (not marked on any maps), above which it continues climbing for 50 metres (**NNE**) through gorse and spiny broom before levelling out to follow the contour lines of the hillside, crossing the **Barranco de Hiniestral** watercourse and joining a firebreak circling a plantation of pine (**Wp.3, 50M**).

We cross the firebreak and take the path through the woods to their northernmost tip, where the path crosses the firebreak again and heads **NE** in a clearly visible line across the last stretch of scrub to the first rock slides. Here the landscape changes character. To the south we see something akin to the pasture-rich Pyrenees; to the north is a facsimile of the stony wilderness found in the High Atlas.

The path becomes fainter, rougher and narrower as it climbs (**NNE**) towards the jagged crags of the **Tajos del Cortadero**, zigzagging through two steep sections and passing a small cairn (**Wp.4, 105M**) before it loses definition beside a green-flanked rivulet just before the **Tajos**.

The main path climbs to the left fifteen metres <u>before</u> this rivulet, but it's difficult to see from below and you might find it easier to bear left <u>at</u> the rivulet, climbing off-path and aiming slightly to the right of the large rock, to reach a shallow col and a clearer path fifty metres later. Turning right on the clear path, we follow it up to the low stone walls behind the *tajos*. The walls (**Wp.5, 130M**) are all that exist of what some maps, with infinite optimism, call the 'Refugio de Lanjarón', a refuge that was in fact never built.

The main path continuing past the 'refuge' is our return route. To climb **El Caballo**, we head north-west (**NW**) from the 'refuge' (off-path but marked by a cairn) gradually bearing north, then north-east, then east, maintaining throughout a discrete distance from the drop into the **Hoya del Zorro**. We eventually join a faintly trodden path up to the peak (**Wp.6, 150M**), from where we can see all the way along to the **Alcazaba** (just to the left of the **Mulhacén**) and can even pick out the main path climbing the **Mulhacén** from **Caldera**.

A clear path descends **NW** to the **Laguna & Refugio de Caballo** (**Wp.7, 165M**) where a bathe is strongly recommended (always supposing your heart's up to it!) (NB bathing in the lagoons is prohibited by the park authorities, a prohibition like most Spanish prohibitions, more often neglected than respected).

The return path heads south from the refuge, passing the eastern face of the **Caballo** and the so-called 'Refugio de Lanjarón' to join the top of the path (clearly visible from above) (**Wp.8, 185M**) down to the rivulet. From here you can return to the firebreak/pine-wood by the same route or take a more adventurous, pathless route along the crest (good visibility preferable).

The off-path route follows the line of the ridge, staying just to the east of the rocky outcrops along the crest, until it reaches an outcrop (**Wp.9, 200M**) from where we can see the length of the ridge and, off to the left, the firebreak/pine-wood. We maintain a southerly (**S**) direction after **Wp.9** until we <u>see</u> a large cairn topping another outcrop of rock in the distance. Bearing left to pass below a long, sloping crag, we aim for the northernmost tip of the firebreak/pine-wood, a twenty to thirty minute descent through broom and furze. Alternatively, cut straight down to the outward path from the firebreak/pine-wood.

Ignoring the path taken through the pine on the way up, we follow the firebreak round the lower part of the wood. When it starts climbing on the southern side of the wood (**Wp.10, 265M**), we take the narrow path on the left down to the *acequia*. We then follow the *acequia* till it crosses the path (**Wp.11, 275M**) down to the **Refugio de Ventura** (just before a small pine tree), from where it's a fifteen minute descent back to the car.

> **Suggested Strolls**
>
> **Lanjarón Valley** – stay on the main path after the **Refugio Ventura** to explore the valley.

13.

CÁÑAR - CERRO MAN - PUENTE PALO - CERRO MAN - (CÁÑAR)

Puente Palo is one of the Alpujarras' better kept secrets, which (being cynical about it) might explain why this *Área Recreativa* is so clean. Apart from local ramblers and a catatonically taciturn shepherd, it's rare to see anyone there - and yet metre for metre, this is perhaps one of the most beautiful walks in the entire Alpujarras, especially between **Wps. 5&8** as it follows the gorgeous **Acequia Grande** under the shade of the finest oak forest in the region. And the miracle of it is, this itinerary appears in no other publication I know of! I can only suppose the want of grandiose views and high peaks means more macho researchers have dismissed it as insignificant. During the summer, the extension between **Cáñar** and **Cerro Man** has little to recommend it, and should only be taken if you don't have a car; it is, however, a lot of fun on a blustery winter's day. The official start of the walk is **Cerro Man**, though it could equally be started from **Puente Palo Área Recreativa (Wp.8)**.

In the following description, **PF2** refers to the main **Pista Forestal 2**, **PF2A** to the **Cáñar** branch.

Though the owner has plans to rebuild, **Cerro Man** is at present no more than a small hump topped with ancient foundations, 4.9km from **Cáñar** on **PF2A**, 3.8 km from the junction with the main **PF2**. The track next to it is flanked by two gate-like stone & concrete walls, marking the passage of the dry **Acequia de Barjas**. It's fifty metres from the point where **PF2A** comes alongside the **Acequia Grande** and just above the junction of the two *acequias*. You can park beside the track at **Wp.1**.

(one way)

*2 | 1** hour | 3 km | 300m **** | 3+

*(3 with the extension)
**(add 1 hour 30 mins return for the extension)
***(add 3 km return for the extension)
****(add 400 metres for the extension)
+(in **Cáñar**, though refreshments <u>may</u> be available when **Cortijo La Muda** is open to the public – see Appendix A, Pista Forestal 2 & Appendix C, Fernando Vilchez)

Extension
Take the concrete lane climbing from the western side of **Cáñar** church. Ignore a rock-laid path climbing left above orange garage doors and take the second path on the left, directly in line with the church tower and just after a concrete building on the right immersed in fig trees. The dirt path soon turns into a mule trail that climbs straight up, cutting across and occasionally disappearing into **PF2A** five times before it reaches **Cerro Man**. For ease of reference these crossings are numbered in brackets in the following section.

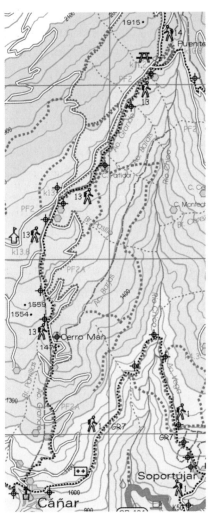

After five minutes we take the access track behind a large fenced *cortijo* to join **PF2A** for the first time (**1**). We bear left here and then again 100 metres later, on a rough track alongside another fenced *cortijo*. Crossing this second *cortijo*'s access track next to a *Prohibido El Paso* sign, we recover the mule trail as it winds up alongside a dry watercourse, to cross **PF2A** (**2**) just below a scattered group of scorched chestnuts, and again 75 metres later (**3**). Immediately after this third crossing the path runs into another access track, climbing past a small house above which it rejoins **PF2A** (**4**). Five metres to the left we recover a paved section of the mule trail, climbing behind a ruin and a small stone cabin. 30 metres behind the cabin we cross **PF2A** for the last time (**5**) and climb straight up, passing between a stand of holm oak on the edge of **PF2A** (on our right) and a long grassy meadow (on our left). The ruins and large threshing circle of **Cerro Man** are 75 metres above the holm oak, 40 minutes (at a rapid pace) from **Cañar**.

From Cerro Man

From Cerro Man (**Wp.1, 0M**), after following **PF2A** for 200m we cross a branch (often dry) of the **Acequia Alta** leading down, on our right, to a line of chestnut trees descending to the **Cortijo las Alberquillas**. 20m later (**Wp.2 3M**), we leave the dirt track and turn left onto a rough path marked by a cairn.

The path climbs parallel to the *acequia* before emerging in a field (probably ploughed) in front of a single-storey cabin set amid newly planted poplar and willow trees. We cross the field and bear left above the house onto a path winding into a small chestnut wood, where it broadens to a rough dirt track, climbing steadily until an easier gradient across another field approaches a junction between the *acequia* and **PF2A**.

We follow **PF2A** for 20m till it bears right and we take a very rough dirt track climbing to the left (**Wp.3, 15M**). This track climbs steadily, gradually bearing back towards the *acequia* to join another, better stabilised track leading to a carefully fenced *cortijo*, where we take the path to the left of the house between the *acequia* and the fence.

We follow this path as it crosses a series of shallow terraced fields and widens to a rough dirt track before climbing gently to rejoin **PF2A** (**Wp.4, 25M**). We then follow **PF2A** past several houses, at the end of which, just where the fence bears right above a large empty reservoir, we leave the dirt track to join a path along the *acequia* (**Wp.5, 30M**).

We now follow the *acequia* path all the way to **Puente Palo**, ignoring junctions with driveways at **Wps. 6 (40M)** and **7 (50M)** until we come to a white-painted house with a well-tended garden. The driveway behind the house brings us up to the denuded platform just south of **Puente Palo Área Recreativa (Wp.8, 55M)**.

This route is so lovely, you'll probably want to return the same way, but if you insist on a circuit, take **PF2** south to **PF2A** (**Wp.9**) and follow **PF2A** back to **Cerro Man (5km** from **Wp.9**).

Suggested Strolls

Take **PF2** to **Puente Palo** and, from the bare slope to the south of the *Área Recreativa* (**Wp.8**), take the chained driveway down to the path on the right of the white-painted house then follow the *acequia* till you reach a wire fence above a reservoir (**Wp.5**), bear right and take the dirt tracks back to the *Área Recreativa*.

Also see Pista Forestal 2

14.

PUENTE PALO - PICO ALEGAS - PUENTE PALO

A relatively easy high-mountain walk though complicated by a section where the path is so badly overgrown that one's obliged to plunge through the overhanging boughs of pine trees. It's well worth the effort, though. The spectacle of the high-peaks is fabulous, the ridge gives an unusual perspective on the **Poqueira Gorge**, **Pico de las Alegas** itself is a lovely, little-visited spot, and the descent enjoys superb views of the **Contraviessa**, the **Sierra de Lújar** and, to the west, the **Axarquia**, all against a backdrop of the Mediterranean. Beware of improvising your own routes up to **Cebollar** (**Wp.16**) – I've tried them all and this remains the simplest! Access via Pista Forestal 2 or Walk 13. Park in the shade on the *pista forestal* to the east of **Wp.1**.

4   320 mins   11 km   950m   0

From the western end of **Puente Palo Área Recreativa** we take the chained dirt track (**Wp.1, 0M**) north (**N**). We follow the track as it climbs steadily through the pine forest, ignoring all branches on the left and taking the third branch (fourth in reality, but the third clear one) on the right (**Wp.3, 35M**).

NB
Beware - the second branch on the right (**Wp.2, 20M**) has precisely the same configuration in relation to the main track as **Wp.3** and crosses the same watercourse lower down to enter the lower half of the **Vivero de los Helechares**. **Wp.3** is distinguished by two dead pines blocking the track after thirty metres and, five metres from the junction, a small cairn and a pine painted with blue waymarks.

The branch track crosses a watercourse to join another dirt track climbing alongside the *vivero*. We bear left, ignoring a branch to the right and cross a rough wire gate to enter the *vivero*. We then follow this track all the way to the river, ignoring all branches and sticking to the main traces all the time.

En route, the track climbs gently towards a stand of sickly looking pine, bringing us within sight of the pale grey walls of the **Cebollar Refuge** and the rocks along the western edge of **Pico Alegas**. Five minutes after the stand of sickly looking pine, the track enters a long S-bend, at the top of which (**Wp.4, 70M**) it levels out: it's worth pausing here to get your bearings for the way up to the refuge.

It looks a relatively simple ascent, zigzagging up the slope before bearing left (**Wp.10**) to cross the pinewood, after which it climbs towards the rocky outcrop above the pinewood (**Wp.15**) where a clear path leads to the refuge. However, the path is very badly overgrown and, if the authorities don't do

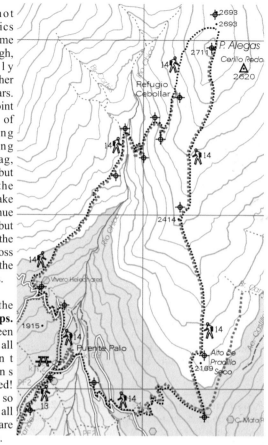

anything or not enough eccentrics like you and me come blundering through, it'll probably disappear altogether in the next few years. The first tricky point comes at the end of the second long leftward bearing stretch of zigzag, where the path all but disappears in the woods (**Wp.9**). Take care not to continue into the woods, but double back to the right in order to cross the wood along the higher line of pines.

N.B. Most of the cairns between **Wps. 6 & 15** have been built by me – all subsequent contributions gratefully received! Because there are so many of them, not all these waypoints are marked on the map.

*Wps.6-15 are timed from the river.

Soon after **Wp.4** the track crosses another wire gate, leaving the *vivero* and descending to the waymarked ford across the **Río Chico** (**Wp.5, 80M**) to join the path up to the woods.

*At the first rocky outcrop 100 metres from the river, we leave the main traces and bear left on a rough path marked by two cairns *(**Wp.6, 3M**) to climb steadily to another cairn (**Wp.7, 5M**) beside a shallow boulder-strewn gully.

We turn left here along a stretch where the path virtually disappears in furze and broom, maintaining a northerly direction to pass just above another cairn and a large rocky outcrop (**Wp.8, 7M**) beyond which a very faint path passes to the right of the first pine and, at another large cairn (**Wp.9, 10M**), doubles-back on the right in a **SE** direction.

After climbing to the left of a few more pines, this very faint path disappears briefly, but soon reappears to climb to another large cairn (**Wp.10, 12M**). The

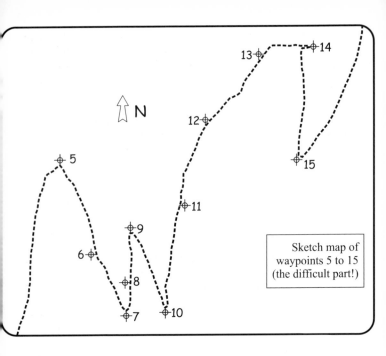

Sketch map of waypoints 5 to 15 (the difficult part!)

clearer path continues in a **SE** direction, but we bear sharp left and go to the right of the next line of pine to cross the pinewood.

The way is often confused and frequently invaded by pine (anyone with a chainsaw in their backpack could make themselves very popular indeed), but if at every apparent Y-junction, you bear right and ALWAYS TAKE THE UPPER TRACES (even when the lower ones seem clearer), you should find cairns at **Wp.11 (19M)** and **Wp.12 (23M)** before emerging beyond the main wood in a shallow gully marked by three cairns (**Wp.13, 27M**).

NB
If there are no cairns when you emerge from the wood, you're probably lower down, in which case you have a very steep climb zigzagging up to the refuge.

At **Wp.13** we bear right and climb straight up the gully (there's no path) then turn right at another cairn (**Wp.14, 30M**) to follow a reasonably clear path climbing gently along the topside of the wood. Just before the rocky outcrop noted at **Wp.4**, we bear sharp left at another cairn (**Wp.15, 33M**) from where we can see the refuge again, a couple of hundred metres ahead.

Unfortunately, there's another small stand of pine to be negotiated, this one devastated by storms and demanding some delicate manoeuvring to clamber over felled trunks, but the way is at least obvious and soon leads to the refuge (**Wp.16, 43M [185M from Wp.1]**), a badly weathered concrete shell but clean enough for sleeping rough, and welcome shelter in bad weather. There's a small spring to the **NW** of the refuge.

Contrary to what some maps tell you, there's no clear path between the refuge and the peak, though there are occasional better trodden sections. Heading in a northerly direction towards the last scattered rocks along the ridge, we gradually bear north-east to join a reasonably clear section through the rocks, though that in turn gradually loses definition before disappearing altogether.

Maintaining a north-easterly direction, we emerge on the ridge 50 metres north of the official peak (**Wp.17, 205M**) and 100 metres south of some stone windbreaks (**Wp.18**) - welcome shelter when the wind's blowing, which it often is, and in any case a cosy picnic spot.

The way back (much simpler than the way up, but a dull climb) follows what's left of the old **Cañada Real (S)**, a dirt track (faint at first but soon becoming clearer) running along the ridge past a series of tall cross-country skiing cairns before descending to merge with a firebreak (**Wp.19, 240M**). After a steady descent, the firebreak climbs a hummock, the **Alto de Pradillo Seco**, just before which another dirt track (**Wp.20, 260M**) bears right to skirt the hummock and join a broader dirt track (**Wp.21, 270M**), which we take to the right, to descend to Pista Forestal 2 (**Wp.22, 310M**) ten minutes from **Puente Palo**.

Suggested Strolls

Short Version to **Wp.5** – Exertion 3 / 2 hours 30 mins return

Also see Pista Forestal 2

---

15. POQUEIRA VILLAGES

The classic tour of the Poqueira villages except for the **Bubíon-Capileira** stretch which takes minor, less well-known paths. An ideal walk for a summer morning, doing most of the climbing while the eastern flank of the valley is still in shade and returning midday for a bathe in the **Poza de Pampaneira**, the swimming pool that the *ayuntamiento* gouge out of the river every July. The views are terrific, particularly on the way down from **Puente Chiscar**.

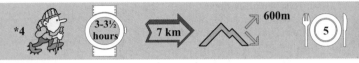

*Full circuit 4, **Pampaneira - Bubíon** 3, **Bubíon - Capileira** 1, **Capileira** to **Puente Molino** via **Puente Chiscar** 3, **Puente Molino - Pampaneira** 3

 Buses back: (from **Capileira**) 3.50 p.m. / 6.20 p.m

Given the maze of **Pampaneira**, a simplified way of finding the start is to begin at the small car-park on the main road at the upper limits of the village. Taking **Calle La Peseta** next to the brown garage doors at the sharp bend below the car-park, we cross the porch of house No. 1 onto **Calle Real** and take the second alley on the left, just before a small *fuente* with a tap and a bench. We then follow this alley past the **Horno del Carmen** and climb to a Parque Natural map board (**Wp.1, 0M**) of a shorter, less comprehensive version of our itinerary.

Shorter versions

Pampaneira - Bubíon - Pampaneira

Pampaneira - Bubíon - Puente Molino - Pampaneira

Bubíon - Capileira - Puente Molino - Bubíon

Bubíon - Puente Molino - Puente Chiscar - Capileira - Bubíon

Capileira - Puente Chiscar - Puente Molino - Capileira

From **Wp.1**, we take the cobbled **Calle Castillo** behind the map board and bear left below house No. 1 onto a dirt path above fields. After 100 metres, we take the upper, waymarked branch and climb steeply to join a dirt track amid the unmistakable stink of a dog pound.

We follow the track to the left for 30 metres then bear right onto an old mule trail. After passing a couple of white water huts and the dry **Barranco de Cerezo**, an increasingly steep climb comes into **Bubíon** on a concrete alley below a *fuente* (**Wp.2, 25M**).

To cross **Bubíon**, we follow the alley up to the church, passing a GR signpost (Pampaneira 30M) and bearing right into the **Plaza de la Iglesia**. We then cross the plaza and take the **Calle Real**. Ignoring a turning on the right, we continue on the concrete lane (**Calle Liso**). At the **Calle Liso** nameplate, we bear left on the paved track down to the football field, above which there is a choice of routes on either side of the **Casa Mariano** (**Wp.3, 35M**).

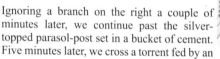

The conventional ramblers' route takes the path down from the black-tipped cross at the corner of the football field, descending via the **Barrancos de Tejar** (a.k.a. **Alguastar**) and **Armuña** (not named on most maps) before climbing to **Capileira** from Wp. ALT. This is the path to take for a simple circuit back to **Pampaneira**, crossing the **Puente Molino** to **Wp.11**. As a route to **Capileira** though, it's plain daft. For a quicker, equally attractive route without losing altitude, we take the broad path to the right of the **Casa Mariano**.

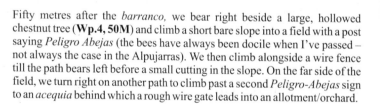

Ignoring a branch on the right a couple of minutes later, we continue past the silver-topped parasol-post set in a bucket of cement. Five minutes later, we cross a torrent fed by an *acequia* then climb briefly before descending to cross the dry **Barranco de Tejar**.

Fifty metres after the *barranco,* we bear right beside a large, hollowed chestnut tree (**Wp.4, 50M**) and climb a short bare slope into a field with a post saying *Peligro Abejas* (the bees have always been docile when I've passed – not always the case in the Alpujarras). We then climb alongside a wire fence till the path bears left before a small cutting in the slope. On the far side of the field, we turn right on another path to climb past a second *Peligro-Abejas* sign to an *acequia* behind which a rough wire gate leads into an allotment/orchard.

Just above this gate, we bear left and cross the *acequia* onto a very narrow path behind the allotment/orchard to follow another *acequia*. Thirty metres after the small house at the end of the allotment/orchard, we leave the *acequia* and take the path (**Wp.5, 60M**) descending on the left to cross an outlet from the *acequia*.

We then take the upper path at the next junction, cross the top of **Barranco de Armuña**, and follow the wall below the 'stepped' flats at the entrance to **Capileira** until we come to a small shady public garden with a couple of disused toilets at its eastern end.

At the western end of the garden, we take the middle of three alleys into **Capileira**, passing the **Casa Museo Pedro Alargon** and the **Cartel de Guardia Civil** to reach a square behind the church, where we bear right up to the **Plaza Calvario** where there's a *fuente*, the **Bar El Tilo**, and the 100-year old lime-tree the bar was named after.

To leave **Capileira**, we take the **Calle del Cubo** at the end of the *plaza* and turn right above the **Apartamentos Vista Veleta** then left onto a partially paved, partially concreted track descending to a Parque Natural noticeboard (**Wp.6, 80M**) immediately after the first right-hand bend. Below **Wp.6**, the track is currently being refurbished. By the time of publication, it should be paved/concreted like the upper section.

If you want to go down to **Puente Molino** (for example, to join Walk 19 or to make a shorter loop), stay on the track after **Wp.6** till you come to the top of the ALT path.

To continue the main walk, we leave the track at the left-hand bend below **Wp.6** and descend to cross a little bridge over a watercourse. We then follow the broad path down into the valley, bearing left at the waypoint junction before crossing the gully below the **Cortijo de la Sacristia** and descending to **Puente Chiscar** (**Wp.7, 100M**).

From **Puente Chiscar**, we take the path climbing (**S**) above the right bank of the **Río Poqueira**, passing a path climbing to the right and a waypost. At a junction marked with 2 wayposts (**Wp.8, 105M**) we take the path on the left, passing behind an abandoned *cortijo* then following an overgrown *acequia* to a little stone hut.

A few minutes later, the path crosses a watercourse and divides, the two branches soon merging just before another watercourse north of the **Barranco de las Rosas**. We bear left at the next junction (**Wp.9, 120M**), cross the second, main watercourse and then follow the level path (ignoring the branch climbing right 50m after the watercourse) out of the *barranco*.

Just before the fallen trunk of a long dead chestnut (**Wp.10, 125M**), we ignore a path climbing to the right and continue straight ahead to descend past a threshing circle and an abandoned *cortijo* to the **Cortijo Enrique**, inhabited by a benignly smiling old man and about 95 madly barking but equally harmless dogs.

We then bear right immediately in front of the

Suggested Strolls

Bubíon-Pampaneira (Wps. 2-1). Buses back: 12.35/2.05/7.20 p.m.

Capileira-Bubíon (top route) (**Wps. 6-3**)

Capileira-Mirador de Aldeire - don't turn left after the **Apartamentos Vista Veleta** in **Capileira** but continue straight ahead on the paved track (**Paseo de Aldeire**) down to the threshing circle *mirador*.

Bubíon-Barranco de Cereza Robledal. Take the path opposite the **Fuenfría Bar** on the main road. Bear right at the first junction and climb to a dirt track. Turn right and descend to the GR7 which leads back into **Bubíon**.

La Poza de Pampaneira. Take **Calle Princesa** from **Pampaneira** car park, pass the **Carnicería Mercedes** and, when you see the **Calle Silencio** sign, turn left to join a concrete track (**Calle Moraleda**) beside a GR7 sign ('Soportújar 2h') and a defaced Parque Natural notice board, from where you can descend to the track (**Wp.15**) to **La Poza** (**Wp.14**).

cortijo, descending to a branch of paths at a watercourse with a small bridge (**Wp.11, 135M**) 100 metres above **Puente Molino**. From **Wp.11**, we bear right again for the last climbs of the day ('climbs' because this is one of those slopes that always have another little incline lying in wait behind the last one).

After a couple of minutes the path dips down into a deepish swale before climbing steeply again. The gradient ameliorates all the better to surprise us with another steep climb up to a burnt out tree, 30 metres after which it crosses the first of three watercourses (the second two are usually dry). After the third watercourse, the path climbs for the last time through a small oak wood to emerge on a grassy field just below a ruin with fine views of all three villages and the **Mulhacén**. Just beyond the ruin, a waypost (**Wp.12, 155M**) marks the way DOWN to **Pampaneira**.

The path descends rapidly, soon presenting us with the encouraging sight of the river and the somewhat less encouraging sight of a decidedly unstable looking tower of rock looming over the path. Shortly after passing (hopefully) the rock tower we turn sharp left at a waypoint (**Wp.13, 165M**) just beyond a roofless ruin, and take a narrower path heading back upriver.

This path soon starts zigzagging down toward the **Poza de Pampaneira**, passing a branch on the right before descending to the last badly-eroded 20 metres, and the bridge just below **La Poza** (**Wp.14, 170M**). After a swim in **La Poza**, we take the dirt track up from the bridge to the bend in the road at the village's lower limits (**Wp.15, 180M**) and bear left to follow the GR7 concrete track into **Pampaneira**.

16.

PAMPANEIRA - PITRES - PAMPANEIRA

A complex route of contrasts, following some very steep stairs, some very tame forestry tracks, and some very rough cross country-walking! The stairway between **Wps. 4&5** is not recommended in the opposite direction unless you take a perverse pleasure in vertigo.

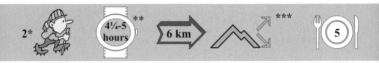

2* 4¼-5 hours ** 6 km *** 5

*5 for the stairs
Pampaneira - Pitres 2 hours 30 mins, **Pitres - Pampaneira** 1 hour 35 mins
  Circuit without **Pitres** 3 hours 15 mins
***from **Pampaneira** - 600m, from **Pitres** - 100m (climb)

 Buses back- from **Pitres** - 3.30 p.m. / 6 p.m.
  from **Pampaneira** - 2.05 p.m. / 7.20 p.m.

Short Version	
turn right at **Wp.9** rather than descending to **Pitres**.	We start as per Walk 15, but stay on the **Calle Real** (**Wp.1, 0M**) up to the cemetery. NB. You could also park here, taking first left off the **Bubíon** road 200 metres after the car-park (see Walk 15).

From **Pampaneira** cemetery, we follow the concrete track till it bears sharp right towards the sports field (**Wp.2, 10M**) and we continue along the dirt track on the left to two large whitewashed reservoirs. Two hundred metres after the reservoirs, shortly before wooden posts carrying a thick woven metal cable, we take the slippery trail climbing to the right (**Wp.3, 15M**) to cross an *acequia* and climb very steeply alongside the buried pipe bringing water to the Central de **Pampaneira**. At the top, we bear left to by-pass a bricked up tunnel and join the **Bubíon** road (**Wp.4, 30M**).

Crossing the road we take, to the right of a small hut with red and yellow dots on its silver metal door, the service stairs alongside the water pipe for a very steep climb. The actual climbing time is probably no more than twenty minutes, but it takes much longer as rest stops are inevitable. At the top of the first flight of stairs, we cross a gentler slope to the second flight which, after considerable heartache, gives way to more widely-spaced concrete and tarmac steps as the gradient eases. If you're still standing when the pipe finally disappears into the holding dam (**Wp.5, 70M**), duck under the pipe (**N**) and follow the faint trail across the mica shale toward a square concrete triangulation post.

The path bears right shortly before the post and climbs to join the GR7 (Walk 3, Wp.3). We bear right here, away from the GR, on a path climbing **SSE** to

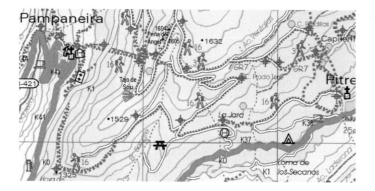

pass below the dam wall and join the dirt track up to the **Tajo de Soju** (see PF3 strolls).

Just before a small metal pylon mounted with **Pampaneira**'s TV aerials (the *mirador* is 200 metres beyond the turning circle behind these aerials), we bear left to follow the track **NE** towards the rocky outcrop of the **Peña del Angel**. On the far side of the **Barranco de la Sangre** (on our right) is the 'graveyard' of concrete pipes (Walk 3, Wp.5), looking curiously like an experiment in installation art from this angle.

The track crosses both the old GR7 (two wayposts, **Wp.6, 85M**) and the new route (Walk 3, Wp.4). You can either cross the **Barranco de la Sangre** here (to Walk 3's Wp.5), or stay on the track past the transformer towers till the Y-junction (**Wp.7, 90M**). At the Y-junction, we turn sharp right to follow the 'Cortijo Prado Toro' signs (**SE**), crossing the GR7 again (Walk 3, Wp.5) after five minutes.

Ignoring all branches, we follow the main track down towards **Prado Toro**. At the next signposted turning to 'Cortijo Prado Toro' (**Wp.8, 105M**), we stay on the main track as it bears right to descend past a second left-hand branch before passing above a vineyard and below a turning on the right (**Wp.9, 115M**). This turning is the return route, which can be taken now for a circuit lasting a little over three hours.

To continue to **Pitres**, ignore branches leading to the vineyard (on the left) and something that looks suspiciously like a tip (on the right), and stick to the main track as it bears left. We leave the track at the sharp right-hand bend round the heliport (**Wp.10, 125M**) and continue (**E**) on a path skirting an orchard to a junction with a dirt track (**Wp.11, 130M**).

We then follow this dirt track (**E**), crossing a torrent (**Wp.12, 137M**) before gradually descending to join the road (**Wp.13, 140M**) down to **Pitres**, arriving in front of the **Disco Pub El Patio** (**Wp.14, 150M**) just short of the bars in the main *plaza*. To return to **Pampaneira**, retrace your steps until **Wp. 9**.

To start from Pitres

If you're starting from **Pitres**, take the road in front of the *alimentación* Spar and climb past the **Pub El Patio**, the school and **Casa Holandesa**. After a steep S-bend, ignore the tarmac road to the right and the driveway on the left, and continue climbing (**W**). After ten minutes, the road bears right above a single-storey concrete house with an *acequia* behind it (**Wp.13**). Leave the road here and take the dirt track on the left, gradually climbing to cross a torrent (**Wp.12**). Ten minutes from the road, after passing two branches on the right, the track reaches a junction (**Wp.11**). Take the broader higher path on the right and go round the orchard to join a major forestry track behind the heliport (**Wp.10**). Climb the track for about fifteen minutes, ignoring a branch to the left just before the *Parque Natural* sign and, 150m after the first sharp right-hand bend, take the track on the left (**Wp.9**, **35 minutes from Pitres**).

To Pampaneira from Wp.9

The clear, well-stabilized track climbs past a large empty reservoir before descending to cross the **Barranco de la Sangre** and climbing again to pass another narrower track doubling back on the right (**Wp.15, 45 minutes from Pitres**) to the GR7. Continue on the main track but don't spend too much time admiring the fine views of the southern *sierras* (though do keep your eye open for a big buck *cabra montés* that's often to be seen round here; deeply puzzled by a human presence, he lets ramblers come quite close) since you need to be alert for path finding here as the itinerary soon leaves the dirt track and descends to a firebreak.

One hundred metres from **Wp.15** the track bears right, away from the **Barranco de la Sangre**; up to our right is a large sail-like rock below which a small outcrop of rock marks the descent from the track. Fifty metres after, the track bears right, just before the sail-like rock (now concealed by holm oak), the track widens slightly and we turn left between (hopefully!) two cairns (**Wp.16, 50M**) onto a very rough bulldozer trail passing between two stands of spindly holm oak (five on the left, nine or ten on right). If the cairns have been destroyed, you might be able to identify the spot by some large pieces of plastic moulding that have been dumped there.

The bulldozer trail bears left and descends on the right of the small outcrop of rock, within sight of the firebreak below. The track gets even rougher (!) and, just after the outcrop of rock, passes a small sturdy pine tree on our left, where the trail gets too steep and slippery for an easy descent. To avoid the indignity of doing this section on your bottom, bear right (**SW**) after the sturdy pine and immediately before a stand of very small holm oaks, and follow the faint goat tracks that head towards two pine trees, one little, one large, after which it's a relatively easy descent to the firebreak (**Wp.17, 60M**).

We then follow the firebreak (**W**) for one hundred metres as it dips below a stand of tall pines. Just as it starts to climb gently, we leave the firebreak to take a narrow goat track (**Wp.18, 62M**) marked by two cairns (please feel free to add a stone) and a forked pine log. We follow this track as it runs parallel to the firebreak above.

Just after two bushy holm oaks, the track splinters. We follow the upper traces which appear to climb slightly towards the firebreak, then duck under the next holm oak where the main path becomes clearer again. After another cairn, the path descends gently, passing below the skeletons of two burned pine trees and, five minutes from the firebreak, above the ruins of a tiny hut, a few minutes from the **Hoya de los Guardas** pass into the **Poqueira** valley (**Wp.19, 70M**).

If you are doing this route in reverse

If you're doing this route in reverse, the climb from the pass to the firebreak is easy to find, but locating the bulldozer traces is tricky as they don't go all the way to the firebreak. Follow the firebreak east (**E**) for one hundred and fifty metres till it starts a gentle descent into the **Barranco de la Sangre** and you can see its continuation climbing the eastern side of the *barranco* above a newly planted vineyard. Just before the firebreak drops dramatically into the valley, you'll see a cairn on an outcrop of rock on your right. Ten metres before that cairn, another larger one on the left marks the bottom of the bulldozer track (**Wp. 20**), which climbs very steeply up to the left of another outcrop of rock, after which the way to the forestry track at **Wp.16** becomes clearer.

From the **Hoya de los Guardas** pass (**Wp.19**), a clear path crosses the flank of the **Monte de Pampaneira** (**NNW**) into the **Poqueira** gorge. After ten minutes, the path passes some beehives and widens into a track descending to the **Bubíon** road. We cross the road and follow the clear goat tracks down to the sports field and the concrete track (**Wp.2**) into **Pampaneira (95M)**.

17. CAPILEIRA - LA CEBADILLA

This is the well-known **Red Route** from **Capileira** to **La Cebadilla**, the abandoned hamlet built to service the Central **Poqueira** power-station at the junction of the **Ríos Toril & Naute**. On the way back, we pass **Puente Buchite**, one of the loveliest picnic spots in the gorge, but get there early if you're visiting in the summer, as it's popular with local expats and guided parties. If it's not your habit already, take a towel. You can park in the municipal car-park or, if you don't fancy negotiating the narrow alley down to the car-park, on the main road one hundred metres above the **Café-Bar Rosendo**.

2	145 mins *	7 km	300m	4 (in **Capileira**)

*+ 20 mins for the extension.

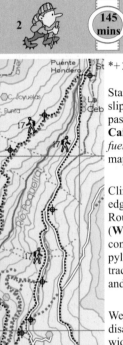

Starting at the northern end of **Capileira**, we take the slip road next to the *Aparcamiento Municipal* sign just past the **Café-Bar Rosendo**, then bear left on the **Caidero de las Ramones** and turn right opposite the *fuente* on a cobbled path with two *Parque Natural* mapboards (**Wp.1 0M**).

Climbing past the mapboards, we cross a dirt track at the edge of the village and take the broad path past a Blue Route mapboard. This path passes two water huts (**Wps. 2&3, 10M & 15M**): after the first hut, we continue up the main path towards the electricity pylons; after the second, we turn left on a narrow dirt track leading to the **Acequia de Lugares** at a waypost and new stone building.

We then follow the *acequia* (which occasionally disappears underground, notably where the track widens near a recently restored *cortijo* [**Wp.4, 40M**]) till a gentle five minute climb leads to **La Cebadilla** forestry track (**Wp.5 50M**). We turn left here and follow the track through **La Cebadilla** to the **Puente Hondero** (**Wp.6, 70M**), passing above a fine bathing spot just after the last buildings on the left.

Extension

From **Puente Hondero**, take the concrete track behind the red and white barrier, cross a second bridge at the junction of the **Ríos Toril** and **Naute**, and a third, **Puente Naute**, to a *Parque Natural* mapboard (see Walk 18). When the path upriver bears left and starts climbing, carry straight on to descend to the river and a pleasant bathing spot, ten minutes from **Puente Hondero**.

To return to Capileira

We take the track climbing south from **Puente Hondero** along the right bank of the **Río Poqueira**. After ten minutes of steady climbing, the track bears sharp right below a *cortijo* (**Wp.7, 80M**). Immediately after the bend, a waypost indicates a narrow path climbing between the main farm buildings and a tall pylon with a small aerial on top. We follow this path between the fields beyond the *cortijo* until it goes to the left of a ruin and joins the **Blue Route**.

Continuing on the lower **Red Route**, we eventually cross a small torrent among poplar trees, where the path divides. The branches soon merge again, but in dry weather it's probably nicer to take the lower path along the stream. Once the paths rejoin, we climb beside a narrow, cement lined *acequia* to a small bridge over another torrent, after which a muddy stretch and a brief climb lead to another *acequia* and waypost (**Wp.8, 95M**).

After another *cortijo*, evidently a goat farm, the path bears round to cross two gates and a *barranco*. We ignore the tracks climbing beyond the *barranco* into a field and continue on the lower path to pass below a small stone cabin/corral and above a ruin.

Suggested Strolls

La Cebadilla-Río Naute
Drive to **La Cebadilla** on the dirt track starting at km 2.7 of Pista Forestal 3, then stroll upriver from **Puente Hondero**.

Capileira-Puente Buchite
From the **Mirador de Aldeire** (see Walk 15 strolls) follow the track down to the branch path to **Puente Buchite**.

Capileira - Acequia de los Lugares - Mirador Aldeire - Capileira
From the *Aparcamiento Municipal* sign in **Capileira**) follow the road up to the picnic spot above the village. Take the dirt track on the left. Bear right at the Y-junction then left to head for the round building. Bear right onto the **Cebadilla** route. Leave the path where two tracks merge next to the **Acequia de los Lugares** and bear left to follow a degraded path (**W**) down a watercourse along a ridge behind a *cortijo* to the tip of the ridge. Thread your way off-path through the rocks to the south to pick up a faint path running up to some fields, then take the narrow path descending to the **Mirador de Aldeire**.

The path then starts winding down towards the river. You'll soon see a stand of poplars downriver and beyond them the path climbing to **Capileira** from **Puente Buchite**, which we reach in thirty minutes from **Wp.8**. Once over the bridge, a scramble across rocks on the left leads into a lovely picnic spot on the riverbank underneath the poplars.

The final climb to **Capileira** follows the stony path up from the bridge, soon passing a waypost (**Wp.9**) marking a branch down to **Puente Chiscar**. We continue on the main path to join the dirt track into **Capileira**, arriving at the **Mirador de Aldeire** threshing circles (**Wp.10, 145M**) after a twenty-five minute climb from the river.

We then follow the paved track, the **Paseo de Aldeire**, into **Capileira**. The alley on the left just before the **Apartamentos Vista Veleta** leads back to the start of the walk, while **Calle del Cubo** in front of the *Apartamentos* brings us up to **Plaza Calvario** and the **Bar El Tilo**.

18. RÍO NAUTE CIRCUIT

This exceptional itinerary is, along with the **Caballo**, our favourite high mountain route. This walk of delicate beauty and sublime grandeur climbs from **La Cebadilla** through land that gets ever wilder with fabulous views, before descending from the **Cámara de Carga** along the *tubería*, the waterpipe feeding the 'Central Poqueira' turbines. What's more, if you're lucky, you may meet Paco 'El Pastor Poeta', 'the Shepherd Poet', who spends his summers at the **Cortijo Toril** with his brother, and is only too happy to regale passers-by with recitals of his poems lamenting the many women who have failed to love him as he would have wished. Access via Pista Forestal 3: turn left at km 2.7 and follow the dirt track down to **Puente Hondero**. If the space is free, park in the shade of the cliffs just west of the *puente*.

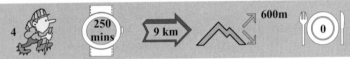

4 | 250 mins | 9 km | 600m | 0

Short Version

Turn back at the bridge over the **Río Veleta** (**Wp.8**) 2h30 return.

From **Puente Hondero** (**Wp.1 0M**), we take the concrete track up to the power station and cross the bridges over the **Ríos Toril** and **Naute** to a mapboard outlining a version of this walk. We then cross the concrete ledge after the mapboard and take the mule trail climbing away from the **Río Naute**.

Ignoring a minor branch on the right five minutes later, we continue climbing using the shortcuts according to taste, haste and lung capacity. One shortcut (emerging at a triangulation post **Wp.2 20M**) has virtually replaced the original route. After a series of zigzags and a long steady climb, the trail levels out just before a branch to the left (**Wp.3, 25M**) climbs to **Puente Toril** (**Wp.17**), our return route.

We continue on the main, level trail, as it dwindles to a dirt path passing a *cortijo*/byre before climbing gently to a second, ruined *cortijo* (**Cortijo Masagrande, Wp.4, 35M**) beside two wayposts, one indicating another path up to **Puente Toril**. We stay on the main path as it descends very slightly to pass immediately behind a white-painted *cortijo*, after which another gentle climb leads up to two large walnut trees, and a wayposted path down towards the river and the **Cortijo de la Isla**, visible on a small rise in the middle of the river.

Bearing left at the top of a rough, boulder-strewn spur, we follow the clear but eroded path down to the rocky right bank of the **Río Naute**. Two small bridges fifty metres below the **Cortijo de la Isla** cross the watercourses defining the island before a third bridge brings us to the *cortijo* itself (**Wp.5 55M**), where the landscape becomes much wilder and greener.

We then follow the path up **La Isla** behind the *cortijo* towards the escarpment of the **Tajo Cañavate**, bearing right after a few minutes to climb over a knoll to another waypost (**Wp.6, 60M**). Another rough bridge crosses the lower reaches of the **Barranco de Cañavate** and, a hundred metres later, yet another bridge leads into a marshy green meadow on the right bank of the main river.

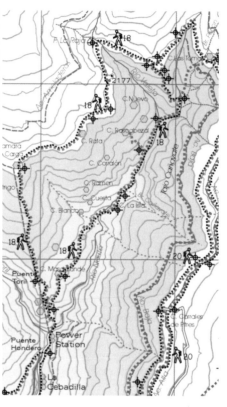

The path gets narrower here and is occasionally waterlogged as it climbs past another ruin, before bearing away from the river into a steeper climb. We zigzag up a rock-laid stretch, ignoring a branch on the right to join a gentler gradient leading to a Y-junction (**Wp.7, 80M**). The path on the left climbs to **Cortijo Rascabezal**, an alternative but much rougher route to the **Fuente La Raja** (**Wp.13**).

We take the wayposted path on the right, descending back towards the river, where the path disappears in a water-logged meadow before re-emerging on the far side, after which it follows the **Río Naute**, passing through successive dry and waterlogged sections before reaching the bridge over the **Río Veleta** (**Wp.8, 90M**).

Beyond the bridge a very narrow path climbs through dense vegetation, briefly following the left bank of the **Río Veleta** before veering back towards the **Naute**. The landscape becomes wilder and drier as the path climbs past occasional cairns before circling a large rocky outcrop to another junction (**Wp.9, 105M**) marked by two wayposts.

The main path on the right leads up to **Cortijo Las Tomas** and the **Poqueira Refuge** (see Walk 20) both of which have been clearly visible for much of the preceding hour. We, however, turn left onto a rough narrow path climbing the rise between the **Ríos Veleta** and **Naute**.

The path climbs steeply, occasionally losing definition, but the route is clearly marked by cairns and concrete triangulation posts. To the left, you'll soon see the concrete installations at **Fuente La Raja** (**Wp.13**), our next objective. Bearing left at the remains of a threshing circle (**Wp.10, 125M**), we follow the cairns till the path bears right at a waypost (**Wp.11, 127M**) where we leave the waymarked route to take a shortcut.

NB
The 'official' route is almost as wild as the shortcut, but if you're doing this in reverse, stick to the official route (via **Wp.L3**, see below) as it's better marked with cairns.

We bear left at **Wp.11** and, fifty metres after the waypost, start climbing a shaley slope past the remains of ramparts that once shored up a path, heading for a sharp rock tipped with a concrete triangulation post. Bearing left ten metres below the triangulation post, we continue climbing towards a large cairn on a rock below the cliffs (**Wp.12, 140M**) where we rejoin the sketchily waymarked route along a rough path below the cliffs. This path follows the underground pipe taking water from the **Río Naute** to the **Fuente La Raja**, **La Cámara de Carga** and, eventually, the **Central de Poqueira**.

As you follow this path, you may care to glance across to the far bank of the **Río Veleta**. A little way above the clear green line of an open *acequia*, you should be able to make out the continuation of the underground pipe from **Fuente La Raja**, the **Ramal del Naute**. Despite the daunting looking pinnacle of rock rising above it (the 2177 metre point on our map), this marks our route. The faint path climbing behind the pinnacle is where we're heading and it's nothing like as horrifying as it looks from a distance. Promise!

Just after the installations at **Fuente La Raja** (a gloriously wild place despite all the concrete) the path divides in front of a tiny hut with a faded green door (**Wp.13, 155M**). Ignore the branch descending on the left to the *acequia* and follow the underground pipe for a hundred metres to an inspection hatch (a stone tower with a concrete lid), ten metres after which, we bear right onto a very rough path marked with cairns that climbs for five minutes to a pass behind the pinnacles.

At first, the path beyond the pinnacles is indistinct, but if you pick your way down the slope for ten metres, you'll soon recover a clear if rough path that passes above a stone water hut. After a brief climb behind the water hut, the path becomes smoother and another gentle climb leads up to a waypost (**Wp.14, 180M**) where it's worth pausing to look back at the distinctive peak of **Veleta**.

The path then bears round the mountain before descending back to the **Ramal del Naute** waterpipe at an inspection hatch five minutes from **Wp.14** (**Wp.15** if you're doing this route in reverse) from where it's easy, level walking all the way to the **Cámara de Carga** and its *tubería*, the unmistakable silver pipe descending to **La Cebadilla**.

The tracks splinter as you near the **Cámara de Carga**. You can either take the shortcut, the first branch on the left, or continue till two cairns (**Wp.16, 200M**), fifty metres from the **Cámara** fence, indicate the main route down to the eastern side of the *tubería*. The path descends parallel to the *tubería*, gradually broadening and tracing long loops to break the descent, before coming directly alongside it and running into a slightly steeper descent down to a well-built wooden bridge, the **Puente Toril (Wp.17, 225M)**, which crosses the *tubería* to join the path to the *cortijos* along the **Río Toril**.

Our path meanwhile bears left at the bridge and zigzags down to a small outcrop of rock tipped with stubby holm oak. We bear right at a large cairn and take the rough but clear path to the right of the outcrop, descending to **Wp.3** from where we follow the outward route back to **La Cebadilla** in a little under half-an-hour.

19.

LA ATALAYA & 0.SEL.LING FROM BUBIÓN

Although the climb is not huge and the terrain is not particularly difficult, this can seem like an unusually tough walk, perhaps because there's plenty of opportunity for getting lost, so you need good pathfinding skills. For the rambler, the main attractions are the magnificent views, but there's also the added interest of visiting the Buddhist centre, built in honour of Osel Hita, the first westerner recognised as a reincarnated lama. The centre is open to visitors between 3 & 6 p.m. Our itinerary does not actually 'visit' **O.Sel.Ling**, but given that this is a spiritual retreat, I suggest timing the walk to cross the premises during official visiting hours. Presumably if you're contemplating the divine, you don't necessarily welcome a bunch of big-booted ramblers blundering through your meditations.

Wps.2-5 and the stretch after **Wp.22** follow Walk 15 in reverse. Using Walk 15, this route could easily be adapted to start from **Pampaneira** or **Capileira**.

From Pampaneira, follow the 'La Poza' stroll then climb to join this itinerary at **Wp.22** (Wp.12 of Walk 15); continue climbing to **Wp.20** and bear right to pick up the short version (see below).
From Capileira, see Wp.6 of Walk 15 to join this itinerary at **Wp.1**.

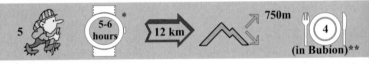

5 | 5-6 hours * | 12 km | 750m | 4 (in Bubión)**

* given the pathfinding problems allow 6 hours walking time

though you might get a free cup of tea from the **O.Sel.Ling students on residential courses if you're lucky

---

Short version
To avoid 90% of the climb, drive to the centre and start from there, or from **Wp.17**. Take Pista Forestal 2 and turn right onto the **O.Sel.Ling** branch setting the odometer at zero. At km 2.3, go left for **O.Sel.Ling** or right for the track below **Wp.17**, after which km 3.5=**Wp.18**, km 4.8=**Wp.20**, and km 5.6=**Wp.10**. Follow the walk as described but stay on the dirt track at **Wp.20** till **Wp.10**. Timing - 2 hours 30 mins. Exertion, 3.

From **Bubión**'s **Plaza de la Iglesia**, we take the **Calle Real**, then the concrete lane (**Calle Liso**) and the paved lane down to the cross at the corner of the football field (**0M**), from where we can see, on the tip of **Atalaya (Wp.14)** to the **SW**, the tiny white speck of the firewatch hut above **O.Sel.Ling**.

We then take the broad path below the football field, passing the **Barrancos de Tejar** (aka Alguastar) and **Armuña** before descending to the **Puente**

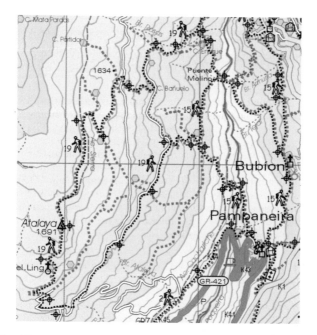

Molino (Wp.1 25M). Crossing the river, we climb to a junction (**Wp.2 30M**), where we turn right and head north to be greeted by smiles and barks (see Walk 15) at the **Cortijo Enrique (Wp.3 40M)**.

Bearing left between the main building and a woodshed, we climb past a ruin and a threshing circle to join another path (**Wp.4 50M**), where we bear right, crossing the **Barranco de las Rosas** to another junction (**Wp.5, 60M**). We then turn left on the orange and turquoise waymarked path and climb back towards the centre of the *barranco* to a small stone and concrete bridge (**Wp.6, 70M**).

After another steepish ascent, we leave the waymarked path as it bears left and take the unmarked path on the right to climb above the *barranco* towards a tall, half dead chestnut tree. Just behind some ruins and a small mulberry tree (**Wp.7, 80M**) the path swings right onto a steep, water-eroded slope where it splits into several goat tracks threading through a wall of *retama*.

We stick to the main track, along which a small scarlet stripe painted on a rock (**Wp.8, 85M**) suggests this is an official route, appearances notwithstanding. Following the main traces, we scramble up a steep scree slope until it emerges onto a flat area (**Wp.9, 100M**) to the right of a dry watercourse and dirt track. There's also a small red dot on a rock to our right and a line of embedded stones forming a channel in the slope ahead.

Bearing left across the dry watercourse, we ignore the grassy track climbing into a field and follow the lower dirt track to pass behind a *cortijo* at the back of which there are four columns topped with orange iron bars. One hundred and fifty metres later we pass below the more substantial **Cortijo Bañuelo** (black metal gates and balustrades, and a magnificent walnut tree). If you glance up just after the **Cortijo Bañuelo**, you'll see a ruined cabin (**Wp.11**) three hundred metres above. This is our next objective.

NB
If the **Cortijo Bañuelo** happens to be unoccupied, immediately after the *cortijo* with columns you can take the driveway up to the **Bañuelo** walnut tree and climb directly behind the *cortijo*. Otherwise, seventy-five metres past **Bañuelo**, a faint path (**Wp.10, 110M**) climbs between an eglantine bush and brambles under a smaller walnut tree.

*If you're coming from the south on the short version, **Cortijo Bañuelo** is the *cortijo* with a solar panel mounted in one corner, one hundred and fifty metres after a line of tin baths in the field on your right.

There's no single path up to the ruin, which disappears briefly as we start climbing, but about halfway between **Bañuelo** and the ruin (visible again), just above the fourth terrace behind the *cortijo*, something akin to a path crosses two more terraces (**SW**) before switching back via a long-abandoned water reservoir to climb to the ruin (**Wp.11, 125M**).

After circling another ancient reservoir behind the ruin, we take a narrow path up to a forestry track twenty metres above the ruin. We turn right on this track, then bear left when another track comes in from the right. You can relax now. Most of the pathfinding problems are past!

Climbing steadily but gently with splendid views over the **Poqueira Gorge** and the **Sierras Lújar** and **Contraviessa**, the track passes a house (**Wp.12, 137M**) on our left and a branch on our right before crossing the **Acequia Nueva** (**Wp.13, 150M**). Ten metres after the *acequia* we leave the main track and take the branch to the left. We follow this branch track as it bears round the mountain and turns into a firebreak then turn left onto another dirt track down to the white-roofed firewatch hut, just beyond the concrete triangulation point marking the **Atalaya** (**Wp.14, 160M**).

We then follow the dirt track past the firewatch hut and, when it bears right (**W**), maintain direction (**S**) to a white-painted concrete post, on the right of which a stony path descends towards (**SW**) a long narrow white flag. If the flag's not flying, aim for a large field with a small stand of oak slightly off-centre and, at its **SE** end, an outcrop of rock where the flag normally is. Ten metres later, and one hundred metres short of the flag, the stony path joins a clearer, grassy path (**Wp.15, 175M**) just above a water-tank with a round metal manhole cover circled in white.

Following the grassy path past the water tank, we pass between the uppermost **O.Sel.Ling** buildings (accommodation for those attending residential courses) onto a dirt track. Following the dirt track down past the showers (water sometimes available) and the camping area, we soon see the 'stupa' (a symbol of Buddha's mind, which apparently resembled a wedding cake) and the coppery roof of a shrine.

At the car-park beside the main entrance (**Wp.16, 180M**), we bear right and follow the dirt track down till a cairn (**Wp.17 205M**) on the left marks a clear path crossing a patch of grass peppered with goat pellets to a large holm oak twenty metres away, where the path drops onto another dirt track and we bear left.

Ignoring the first two branches on the right, we follow the main track which climbs gradually before passing behind a large recently built byre. The gradient gets slightly steeper then eases off again alongside older cabins and byres. Thirty metres after a large oak on the right, we bear right on another dirt track (**Wp.18, 220M**) with a very faint red paint mark on a rock on the left after four metres.

We then follow this track as it climbs very slightly, passing a branch on the right forty metres later and another on the left (**Wp.19, 230M**) that climbs to a white-painted house in the distance. Ignoring a second track up to the white-painted house, we follow the main track as it descends past a recently fenced field.

Eventually, the track curves round another broader flatter field running up to a ruin; just as it starts to climb again, we turn right on another track (too rough to be a *pista forestal*, too broad to be a path) (**Wp.20, 240M**) and descend (**SE**) towards some oak trees. There's also a tiny red dot two metres down this track.

One hundred and fifty metres later this rough track bears sharp left and then winds down above a stone cabin, where it dwindles to a path. To the north of the cabin, a narrow path (**Wp.21, 255M**) comes in from our left. DO NOT take this path. If you do you may well end up on **Pico de Alegas**!

We stay on the same path we've descended as it bears round below the cabin and continues descending to a small ruined *cortijo*. 5m after the ruin, we bear left onto a path (**Wp.22, 258M** [WP12 of Walk 15]) crossing the grassy area below. After the grassy area, the path crosses a small oak wood and three watercourses (the first two usually dry) before making its definitive steep descent to **Puente Molino**, fifteen minutes from the ruin and thirty minutes from **Bubíon**.

20.
POQUEIRA REFUGE VIA THE ACEQUIAS

A glorious, easily accessible high-mountain walk taking one of the traditional routes to visit the impressive **Poqueira Refuge** and returning by the path alongside the **Acequia Alta**. If you want to have lunch at the refuge, make sure you arrive before 3 p.m. as the kitchen is closed between 3 and 5.30 p.m..

4/5*   310 mins **   14 km   500m   5 ***

*   to **Cortijo de las Tomas** 2, to **Poqueira Refuge** 4/5

**   to **Cortijo de las Tomas** 1h50 (one-way)
to **Cortijo de las Tomas**, returning by the *acequia* 4 hours
to **Poqueira Refuge** 2 hours 45 mins (one-way)

***   (at the **Poqueira Refuge**)

> **Short Versions**
>
> Return from **Cortijo de Las Tomas** without climbing to the refuge (see text).
>
> Take the dirt track or the *acequia* back from **Corrales de Pitres**.

To reach the start of the walk, take the **Hoya del Portillo** road from **Capileira** (Pista Forestal 3), setting your odometer at zero when you leave the tarmac. At km 2 the road bears sharp right and we turn left onto a dirt track just after a nicely restored *cortijo*. Eight hundred metres along the track, park at the triangular chimney wall of an unfinished house just before the **Acequia Baja** (**Wp.1**). If you don't have a car, you can ask the Parque Natural bus from **Capileira** to drop you off at the 2 km turning. If you're walking in winter and there's a risk of snow, park at the end of the tarmac.

One hundred metres after crossing the **Acequia Baja** we turn left on another dirt track (usually chained off) which soon brings us in sight of the **Poqueira Refuge** below the **Mulhacén**. A little under one kilometre from the chimney, the track goes through a sharp right-hand bend then swings back north. Just before it bears right again, we take the faint path (**Wp.2, 15M**) on the left below some rocks.

The path soon becomes clear, winding along the contour lines and crossing a series of watercourses until it joins a broader, waymarked path (**Wp.3, 40M**) climbing from **Capileira** (an alternative return route if you came by bus, though bear in mind it's a 600 metre descent from here to **Capileira**).

After crossing a torrent a few minutes later, we continue along the waymarked path to the goat pens at the **Corrales de Pitres** (**Wp.4, 55M**) where the dirt track we left at **Wp.2** ends and a lot of barking begins. Passing below the stone cabins and ignoring the track climbing to the right, we follow the waymarked

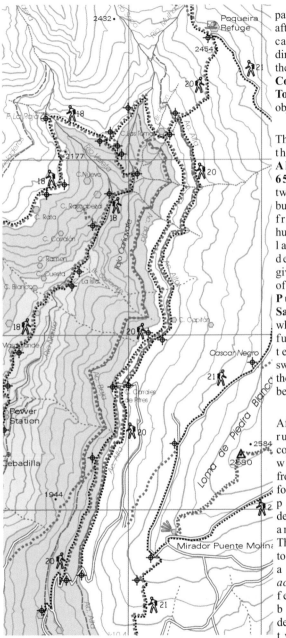

path to the left, after which we can see in a direct line below the refuge, the **Cortijo de Las Tomas**, our next objective.

The path joins the **Acequia Alta (Wp.5, 65M)** beside two wayposts, but bears away from it one hundred metres later for a descent that gives fine views of the **Picos de Pulpito** and **Sabinar**, which when seen from further away tend to be swallowed up by the higher peaks behind them.

After passing a ruined stone corral with two wayposts in front of it, we follow the main path and descend to cross a meagre torrent. The path climbs to run alongside a narrow *acequia* for a few metres before descending past two more wayposts and crossing another torrent, eventually climbing slightly to the **Cortijo de las Tomas (Wp.6, 110M)** from where there are magnificent views down the gorge towards the **Sierra Lújar**.

So far we've only climbed about one hundred metres. If you don't fancy the steep climb to the refuge (400 metres straight up) you could turn back here. However, I recommend a visit to the refuge and strongly recommend climbing to the **Acequia Nueva** for the return. If you came on the bus and feel adventurous, you might wish to tackle one of the very long descents to **Capileira** via the **Rio Naute** and **La Cebadilla** (see Walks 17 & 18).

To climb to the refuge, we take the signposted path behind the *cortijo* (**NE**). After trudging up the first couple of hundred metres, we hop over the **Acequia Alta** (**Wp.7, 120M**) and continue trudging (there's no other word for it). The refuge is, distressingly, out of sight, but the path is clear and well-marked with cairns, so there are no path-finding problems and you can concentrate on your trudging.

After a little over thirty minutes of remorseless trudging, we bear left to cross a marshy area and follow the path winding up through a rocky area dotted with so many cairns it looks like the site of a lunar cult. The object here is to cross the **NW** tip of the rocky ridge that has loomed above us throughout our trudge. Beyond the ridge a waypost marks the last thankfully gentle climb to the refuge (**Wp.8, 165M**), where somebody has thoughtfully built a cement climbing wall on the porch!

The **Poqueira Refuge** (Tel: 958 343 349) is well worth the trudge. It's solidly built, magnificently appointed, immaculately kept, and has excellent dormitory facilities, hot showers, a self-access kitchen, and a complete bar and restaurant service – and you need restoring after your trudge. It's also a good place to stay a few nights for exploring the higher peaks. The guides running the refuge can give you the appropriate information. If you want to stay over, they do have blankets and sell disposable sheets, but it's best if you bring your own sleeping bag..

To return, we take the same route back to the **Acequia Alta**, a thirty minute descent that is easier than coming up but hard on the knees, then follow the path alongside the *acequia*. This is a lovely grassy path lined with foxglove, forget-me-nots, wild lavender, peppermint and the occasional orchid, passing innumerable plunge-pools and accompanied by waters that babble, chuckle and gush according to the depth and slope of the channel. The only drawback is that it's narrow and rough, so you have to watch your feet and are obliged to stop if you want to admire the views. I wouldn't recommend it in winter or when the ground's slippery. Hopefully you won't happen on a day when the water's diverted early, as a dry *acequia* loses nine tenths of its charm.

It's hard to get lost following an *acequia*, but note the following Waypoints:
(**Wp.9, 240M**) we briefly rejoin the outward path (see **Wp.5**).
(**Wp.10, 250M**) we cross the dirt track above the **Corrales de Pitres**, after which an overgrowth of eglantine obliges us to drop down occasionally on goat tracks. Beware of irrigation gates concealed by marsh grass.
(**Wp.11, 290M**) we rejoin the **Corrales de Pitres** dirt track two minutes above **Wp.2**, 20 minutes from **Wp.1**.

21.

The **Mulhacén** is the highest mountain on the Iberian Peninsula and therefore a must for many visitors. This circuit is intermittently waymarked and poses no serious orientation problems. It's not the most interesting ascent, but it is the most practical day trip. For the most part it's an easy walk along clear dirt tracks, however it is very, very long and the final climb to the peak is very steep. The park leaflet claims it takes seven hours, I timed it at eight-and-a-half, but given the length and height climbed, you should allow up to twelve hours counting rest-stops.

This route is included as the most practical single-day circuit to the top. But the descent is a bit boring! If you have the option of being picked up at the end of the day and have good pathfinding skills, or have already done Walks 18 & 20, I recommend taking the bus from **Capileira** to the **Mirador de Trevélez**, following either of the Short Versions to the top, then descending via the **Caldera** and **Poqueira** refuges and the **Río Naute** to **La Cebadilla**. Beware though: the link path crossing the headwaters of the **Naute** from **Cortijo de las Tomas** is a little vertiginous and involves crawling on hands and knees for a couple of metres (see Walk 18).

If you walk the route in winter

The **Mulhacén** can be climbed in winter, particularly in February when the weather tends to be more stable, but given the steepness of its western face, I'd recommend using our descent route as the ascent and coming back the same way. Length might also dictate an overnight stay at the **Poqueira Refuge**. Snow may make the **Hoya del Portillo** start inaccessible as late as Easter, in which case you could park at the firebreak at km 8.9 on PF3 and start climbing from there to pick up the described walk at **Wp.3**.

Walking the route in summer

In summer, late July, early August are the best times, before the electric storms begin. The most likely problem you'll have with the weather is wind, though snow can stay on the peak as late as August. The problem with a summer ascent is that, by the time you get to the top, heat will have hazed the views for which the peak is so justly renowned. The only way round this is to camp out at the **Refuge Caldera** and climb early in the morning. Summer temperatures are pleasant at this altitude, but the UV is very intense: sun-hat, sunglasses, sun-cream are ESSENTIAL; long sleeves/trousers recommended. Water is available at the **Refuge Poqueira**, but has such a vile taste it's best to bring your own.

Several dirt tracks are used here. I use the local name for the main one, the **Carretera de Veleta** (PF3 after the chain).

The short version (see below) from the **Mirador de Trevélez/Alto de Chorillo** is only possible in summer, when the park authority bus drops ramblers off in the morning and picks them up in the evening. Enquire at the

Information Office in **Capileira**. **Hoya del Portillo** is the point to which private cars are allowed. Only the early and late buses go to the **Mirador de Trevélez**. However, all buses go to the new *mirador* being constructed at **Puerto Molina**. Book the **Mirador de Trevélez** bus in advance (Tel: 686 414 576); at the height of the season it can be booked up for several days ahead.

Timing:
Given the sheer length of this walk, I've broken times up for easier reference
Hoya del Portillo – **Poqueira Refuge** 2 hours 10 mins
Poqueira Refuge – **Caldera Refuge** 2 hours 10 mins
Caldera Refuge – **Mulhacén** 1 hour 10 mins
Mulhacén – **Hoya del Portillo** 3 hours 5 mins

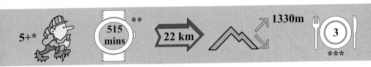

*   Full Walk 5+ (though to be honest, length and altitude send it off the
        scale) It's not difficult but you need a lot of stamina.
        Short Version via the **Loma de Mulhacén**: 4
        Short Version via **Caldera:** 5

**   Full walk 8h35
        Short Version 4h

***   (at the **Poqueira Refuge** - a lower rating than in Walk 20 as it comes too
        soon in this itinerary to be really useful)

🚌   Buses back - see Short Version.

Hoya del Portillo – Poqueira Refuge   2 hours 10 minutes (130M)
From the barrier at the end of Pista Forestal 3 (**Wp.1, 0M**), we take the path to the left of the control hut up to the Guadi-like grottoes and information centre. On the right of the white-painted building, we take the waymarked path up through the pine forest to a firebreak (**Wp.2, 25M**). We then follow this path until it turns left and crosses the firebreak at **Puerto Molina** (**Wp.3, 30M**) between two small waymarks and two tall (currently 'signless') signposts. We cross the firebreak and take the broad dirt track west.

The track descends slightly before bearing right and levelling out. Ignoring a minor branch on the left (**Wp.4, 50M**), we stick to the main track climbing gently towards the **Cascar Negro** quarries. At the first quarry, when the track bears right, we turn left onto a broad, waymarked path (**Wp.5, 60M**) that soon widens to a dirt track climbing past another extraction site.

This track levels out for a long rather dull haul to the junction with the dirt track to the **Poqueira Refuge**. Four hundred metres before the two tracks join, we take the waymarked shortcut on the left to the **Poqueira** track (**Wp.6, 100M**). We bear left on this track then right behind the rocky outcrop and stone byre to descend to the **Poqueira Refuge** (**Wp.7, 130M**).
Poqueira Refuge – Caldera Refuge 2 hours 10 minutes (130M)

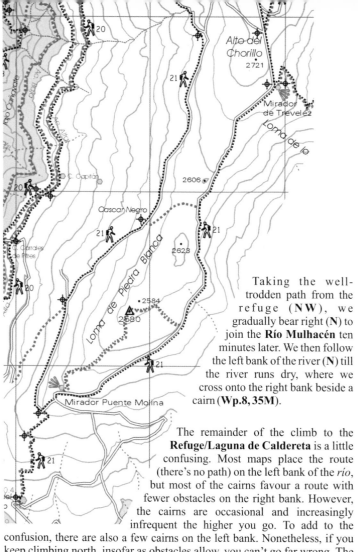

Taking the well-trodden path from the refuge (**NW**), we gradually bear right (**N**) to join the **Río Mulhacén** ten minutes later. We then follow the left bank of the river (**N**) till the river runs dry, where we cross onto the right bank beside a cairn (**Wp.8, 35M**).

The remainder of the climb to the **Refuge/Laguna de Caldereta** is a little confusing. Most maps place the route (there's no path) on the left bank of the *río*, but most of the cairns favour a route with fewer obstacles on the right bank. However, the cairns are occasional and increasingly infrequent the higher you go. To add to the confusion, there are also a few cairns on the left bank. Nonetheless, if you keep climbing north, insofar as obstacles allow, you can't go far wrong. The route described here is the one on the right bank, bearing away from the river to avoid the steeper, rougher stretches. The walking is easier, but the pathfinding is harder. If you're doing the itinerary in reverse, it's best to follow the course of the river where the cairns are better placed for those approaching from above.

A steady climb following the cairns (**NNE**) comes out a little to the east of the **Laguna Majuno (Wp.9, 90M)**. After bearing right alongside the marshy area feeding the lagoon, we climb a shallow stony depression (**N**) between a rocky outcrop and the **Carretera de Veleta**, which is clearly visible 100 metres above.

This depression leads into a grassy swale which we follow towards the centre of the *cirque* defined by the **Mulhacén** and the **Puntal de la Caldera**, crossing another (probably dry) lagoon onto the *carretera* (**Wp.10, 125M**). Crossing the *carretera*, we maintain direction to reach the unmanned but well-maintained **Caldera Refuge (Wp.11, 130M)** overlooking the lagoon.

Caldera Refuge – Mulhacén 1 hour 10 minutes (70M)
East of the refuge, the main path up to the peak is clearly visible. About halfway up, another narrower path comes in from the left. This is the path to take for a slightly gentler start to the ascent.

Following the faint path east from the refuge, we cross a brief pathless stretch over rocks before recovering the trodden way above the splendid jagged cliffs on the northern face of the **Mulhacén**.

After the two paths join (**Wp.12, 30M**), comes the really testing bit - straight up through the most modestly sketched zigzags to the peak (**Wp.13, 70M**), which will probably be relatively crowded, both with Spanish hikers (who are always ready to share their expertise on their favourite local mountains) and *cabra montés* so blasé about human beings, they're almost domestic.

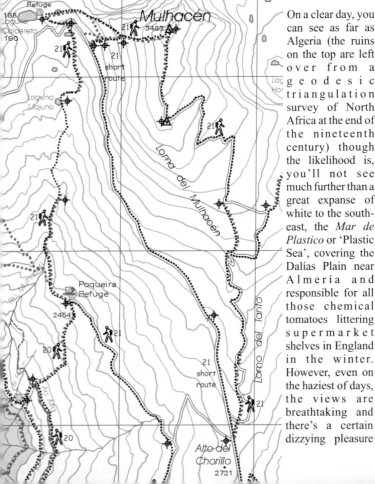

On a clear day, you can see as far as Algeria (the ruins on the top are left over from a geodesic triangulation survey of North Africa at the end of the nineteenth century) though the likelihood is, you'll not see much further than a great expanse of white to the south-east, the *Mar de Plastico* or 'Plastic Sea', covering the Dalías Plain near Almería and responsible for all those chemical tomatoes littering supermarket shelves in England in the winter. However, even on the haziest of days, the views are breathtaking and there's a certain dizzying pleasure to be had from peering over the cliffs to the north, down to the **Laguna de la Mosca**, 500 metres below, a climb some demented enthusiasts undertake in winter when it's a wall of ice – not always with ropes either!

Mulhacén – Hoya del Portillo 3 hours 5 minutes (185M)

The descent is easy, but dull and very, very long. We start along the ridge to the south, along a clearly trodden path that soon joins a stony dirt track laid at the time of geodesic survey and currently neatly covered with blocks of rock in an attempt to regenerate the natural landscape. The track bears left just before a cluster of rock-shelters/windbreaks and another triangulation post (**Wp.14, 15M**) sometimes known as **Mulhacén II**, from where we have clear views of the way back to the **Hoya del Portillo**.

Whether you follow the track all the way down to **Alto de Chorillo** or take the shortcuts (notably **Wp.15, 45M** marked by a cairn), is a matter for you and your knees to come to an arrangement over, but as a general rule, the lower we go the easier and more inevitable the shortcuts seem. Taking the shortcuts, we join the **Carretera de Veleta** a few hundred metres south of the end of the track from **Mulhacén**.

We then follow the *carretera* south, passing the junction with the Poqueira track and signs saying 'El Chorillo' (**Wp.16, 95M**) and the 'Mirador de Trevélez' (**Wp.17, 105M**) where the bus stops.

We then continue along the *carretera* past the small peaks of the **Loma de Piedra Blanca** (it takes 'forever', in reality a little under an hour) until it eventually goes through a U-bend round the new *mirador* (currently under construction), below which we leave the *carretera* and take the firebreak down to **Puerto Molina** and the path (**Wp.3**) through the pine forest to **Hoya del Portillo** (185M).

SHORT VERSION

Take the eight o'clock bus from **Capileira** to the **Mirador de Trevélez/Alto de Chorillo** (WpS.1, 0M), follow the **Carretera de Veleta** (NNW), ignoring branches to left (**Poqueira Refuge**) and right (**Loma de Mulhacén**) before passing a second red-and-white barrier (**WpS.2, 25M**). A few-hundred metres before the **Caldera Refuge**, take the clearly trodden path on the right (**WpS.3, 75M**) up to join first the main path from the *carretera* (**WpS.4, 83M**) then the minor path from **Caldera** (**Wp.12**).

If the **Mulhacén** is still under snow, take the **Loma de Mulhacén** branch of the track for both the ascent and descent.

Suggested Strolls

Hoya del Portillo pine forest - follow the main walk to **Puerto de Molina** (**Wp.3**) and return via the **Carretera de Veleta**

Puerto de Molina - Loma de Piedra Blanca. Take the bus to **Puerto Molina** and, starting on the faint path behind the *mirador*, follow the ridge (**NE**) for twenty-five minutes to **Prado Llano**, distinguished by a concrete triangulation post and stunning views. Head east along faint tractor-tracks to take the **Carretera de Veleta** back to **Puerto Molina**.

22.

PÓRTUGOS JUNTA DE LOS RÍOS

Pórtugos – AR Río Bermejo – (ext. Haza del Cerezo) – Capilerilla – Pórtugos

A pleasant walk through the oak forest above the **Tahá** climbing to an exceptional site, the dramatic cleft in the rock where the **Barrancos del Chorrera** and **Jabalí** converge to form the **Río Bermejo** - take your towel. If you don't like pathless slopes and unstable footing, ignore the extension. Either park in **Pórtugos**, at the western end of **Plaza de la Iglesia** or in the **Plaza Nueva**, or where the walk actually starts, at the top of the concrete track climbing from the petrol station.

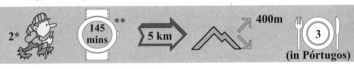

2* | 145 mins ** | 5 km | 400m | 3 (in Pórtugos)

* 3 with the extension
** +30 mins for the extension

From **Pórtugos Plaza de la Iglesia**, we take **Calle Abulagillas** next to the **Productos Carnicos Moises**, then turn right to pass the **Jamones Casa Juan** and cross **Plaza de Churriana**, leaving the village via **Calle Rosario**, which bears right off **Calle Churriana**.

Once out of the village, we follow the track to the white cross (**0M**), one hundred metres after which we bear right up a partially concreted track. We follow this track, ignoring all branches until, fifty metres after the second stretch of concrete, the main track bears sharp right and we take the branch on the left. Since several 'tracks' appear in the next few minutes, I'll call this branch the *pista forestal*.

When the *pista forestal* crosses an *acequia* below a large, cement walled house (**Wp.1, 15M**), we take the rough, unmarked path climbing above the *pista forestal*. We cross the driveway to the house and, when the path rejoins the *pista forestal* a couple of minutes later, bear left on a rough track through the forest.

When this track in turn rejoins the *pista forestal*, we follow the *pista forestal* for fifty metres and take another rough track through the forest on the left. After crossing the *pista forestal* for the third and last time, we take another rough track through the woods, which soon joins a waymarked path (**Wp.2, 30M**), which we follow all the way to the *Área Recreativa*.

After passing an almost sheer outcrop of rock (**Wp.3, 35M**), the path gets stonier and steeper. We bear left when the path joins a rough dirt track, which climbs to the *Área Recreativa* (**Wp.4, 45M**).

Apart from what nature furnished, the *Área Recreativa* doesn't have a lot to recommend it since most of the infrastructure is unused, except for a green rubbish bin that's generally surrounded by a small mountain of refuse, some of it apparently animate. But don't let this put you off. Nature compensates admirably. The views are good and, to the left of the rubbish bin, a path winds down to a spectacular waterfall at the source of the **Río Bermejo**. On a hot day a shower is irresistible.

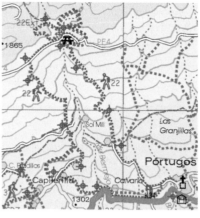

After refreshing ourselves here, we return to the *Área Recreativa* and continue on the dirt track up to Pista Forestal 4, where we turn left and, ignoring a dirt track doubling back on the right, follow PF4 to the bridge over the **Junta de los Ríos** (**Wp.5, 55M** not shown on the map due to the proximity of **Wp.4**).

Extension

Turn right just after the bridge. Ten metres after a waypost with a black arrow on it, turn left on a rough 'way' (I hesitate to call it a path) marked with a blue paint arrow. Follow the ancient, thickly painted waymarks over the rocks to a natural 'jacuzzi' (**Wp.6, 10M** from the bridge) between two waterfalls. Follow the waymarks, climbing past successive waterfalls to their source at the end of the **Acequia Baja** from the **Río Mulhacén**. Bear left under a large pine tree to the point where the *acequia* emerges from a large underground pipe, above which there's a track marked with black-arrowed wayposts. Go down the track one hundred metres (**SSW**), then turn left at another waypost onto a shaley path descending above a firebreak (**E**). The path bears **SW** for a while before swinging back (**NE**) towards the **Barranco del Jabalí** and descending to the waypost beside the bridge (**Wp.5**).

To return to Pórtugos from Wp.5, 55M

Passing above a natural mirador thirty metres from the bridge, we follow Pista Forestal 4 (**W**) for four hundred metres until two small cairns mark the narrow path (**Wp.7, 65M**) down to **Capilerilla**, waymarked yellow five metres lower down. The path winds down through the forest passing occasional waymarks and the odd patch of water-erosion until it follows a stretch of concrete piping (**Wp.8, 75M**) onto an exposed spit, just below which there's a waymarking post.

The waymarked path descends steadily, edging back towards the *río* before widening into a rough forestry track that joins another, better stabilised track above the **Acequia Ventajas Real** (**Wp.9, 95M**) where there maybe a signpost indicating 'Bubíon 1h30 / Pitres 1h' though this was uprooted and propped against a tree last time we passed. There's definitely a nice picnic spot though and another 'natural jacuzzi', twenty metres above the weir (to your left) on the southern side of the *acequia*.

To descend to Capilerilla

We cross the *acequia*, either by the ford or the weir. Ignoring the track on the right, we take the broad path descending through chestnuts, soon passing an eccentrically restored stone house, gaily painted and with Gaudiesque window frames.

The path narrows and bears left along another *acequia*, soon coming into view of the large house on the other side of the **Río Bermejo (Wp.1)**, before crossing the *acequia* four times and emerging on a dirt track above a new house (**Wp.10, 105M**).

This track rapidly descends to the eastern limit of **Capilerilla (Wp.11, 110M)** where, due to private property and the configuration of the **Río Bermejo**, the official route chooses to follow the road to **Pórtugos** 1.5 kilometres away. It's not possible to avoid all the road, but we can skip about two thirds of it.

Fifty metres before **Wp.11**, just after a recently built byre and a small unrestored *cortijo* with two chestnut trees, one with its roots exposed by erosion, we turn left onto a path that doubles back below the *cortijo* then follows an *acequia* to a junction at a stone wall (**Wp.12, 120M**).

Suggested Strolls

Capilerilla - Las Lomillas From the village limit sign on the road down to **Pitres**, take the track on the left (**Wp.11**), then first left up another dirt track. Take the path on the right at the first left-hand bend then bear right at a Y-junction and take the tiny path immediately behind a venerable chestnut tree with partially exposed roots. Follow the faint paths climbing across terraced fields to a terrace with a small platform at the far end with metal poles supporting a sun-shelter and (possibly) a white caravan at the near end. Bear right at a narrow, recently dug irrigation channel and cut across the embankment to join the main walk down (a little below **Wp.9**).

Also see Pista Forestal 4

Turning right with the *acequia* (possibly in it!) then left after fifteen metres, we descend, at first gradually then somewhat precipitously, to the road just before the bridge over the **Bermejo (Wp.13, 130M)**.

To avoid the dangerous bend just after the bridge, we take the slip path on the left, climb up to the **Secadero de Jamones Casa Juan**, then take the drive back down to the road. To finish the walk, we follow the road past the turning to **Atalbéitar** and turn left at the **Pórtugos** petrol station (**Wp.14, 140M**) onto a concrete, lamplit track up to **Calle Rosario**.

23. TAHÁ 1

The **Tahá de Pitres** was the local centre of the medieval silk trade, and still bears the marks in the abundance of mulberry trees off which the silk worms fed, and in the very name **Tahá**, an Arabic administrative district. It's famous for idyllic paths (in a region already famous for idyllic paths), exceptionally pretty villages (ditto), and stunning landscapes (ditto). After the touristy villages of the **Poqueira**, the **Tahá** is a welcome relief. Admittedly, it suffered like everywhere else from the sixties and seventies exodus to the industrial cities of the north and there are plenty of expats buying houses here, but the general atmosphere is still distinctively Alpujarran.

This particular walk threads its way through the higher villages of the **Tahá**, climaxing with the finest *mirador* in the valley, **La Mezquita**. The route follows the GR7 from **Pitres** to **Busquístar** and the GR-142 from **Busquístar** to below the **Mezquita**, completing the circuit with local trails. Most of it is waymarked and the walking is easy apart from the scramble up to the **Mezquita**. Park along the main road (gr-421) through the lower part of **Pitres**.

If you want to avoid slogging back up the road from **Atalbéitar** to **Pitres**, start from **Atalbéitar**. You could also easily start from any of the other villages. If you just want to visit the **Mezquita**, start from **Atalbéitar** and turn right at **Wp.4**.

NB
The cartography identifies the highest point of the ridge between **Wps.11 & 12** as the **Mezquita**. For the sake of ease and in accordance with local custom, I use 'the Mezquita' to refer to the ruins (**Wp.11**) at the tip of this ridge.

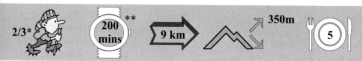

2/3*   200 mins**   9 km   350m   5

*   2 if you take the Walk 24 option at **Wp.10**, 3 if you climb the **Mezquita**.

**   NB
My timings seem much quicker than the official timings with the bizarre exception of the **Pórtugos-Busquístar** stretch where I took considerably longer! The official timings may have been done by different people, or just guessed at. In any case, the domesticity of the landscape means timings are less important for route-finding.

From the main road through **Pitres**, fifty metres above the **Hotel/Restaurant San Roque** and opposite a sign for the Youth Hostel, we take the concrete alley descending next to a GR7 waypost (**Wp.1, 0M**).

The concrete alley soon narrows to a dirt path passing under a tiny aqueduct beside the youth hostel/refuge, immediately after which two branches (**Wp.2 5M**) descend to cross the **Río Bermejo**. The official GR7 route bears right and descends to a bridge. But for a less steep descent, we bear left, cross the little bridge over the *acequia* and, after a slightly larger bridge over a watercourse, take the path on the right down to the **Fuente Agria de Pitres** (an attractive plunge pool and tiny *fuente*), beyond which a narrow path past a ruined mill rejoins the GR7.

The GR7 then climbs towards electricity pylons where it broadens to a dirt track joining the road to **Atalbéitar (Wp.3, 15M)**. Ten minutes on the road leads us down to the outskirts of **Atalbéitar**, where we pass the GR7 sign (Pitres 40') and Wp.1 of Walk 24. We cross the village via the **Calle Real**, the **Plaza Candelaria** and the **Calle El Horno** to emerge above the *lavadero* at the end of Walk 24, where we continue on the broad path heading east, signposted 'Pórtugos 30''.

After passing two stone huts, we climb to the bridge over the **Barranco del Castañar** and a junction of paths (**Wp.4 30M**). The path on the right is the return route and an option for a shorter walk from **Atalbéitar** to **La Mezquita**. For **Pórtugos**, we turn left and climb alongside the *barranco* on an old mule trail till it joins a new dirt track (**Wp.5, 35M**).

We bear left here, then right fifty metres later, where a junction dips into the *barranco*. From here you can see the large white block of the **Hotel Nuevo Malagueño** in **Pórtugos**. When the track swings right, we continue past a large chestnut tree to pick up the old mule trail again.

After a steepish climb along the mule trail, ignoring all the branches into fields, we bear left just below the road. The path crosses an evil looking effluent pipe, passes below the hotel garden and, judging by the bottle caps cobbling the path, the bar, too, before bearing right to join the main road (**Wp.6, 50M**) at a GR7 signpost ('Atalbéitar 30'').

We then cross the road and follow the concrete alley climbing into **Pórtugos**, taking the third turning on the right (at house No. 9) into the **Plaza de la Iglesia**. We continue on the main street through the **Plaza Nueva**, passing the **Hostal/Bar Mirador**. After bearing right out of the **Plaza Nueva**, we leave the main street, turning left in front of the Telefonica installations onto the concrete track signposted 'Busquístar 15''.

The track soon turns to dirt before descending to the road, which we'll follow for the next 500 metres. If you haven't yet tasted the ferruginous waters of the **Tahá**, it's worth pausing at the **Fuente Agria** next to the *ermita*, just after we join the road.

After the *fuente*, the road goes through a long bend to the right before joining a straight avenue of plane trees, at the end of which (**Wp.7, 70M**), we take the broad path climbing to the left just before the road itself bends sharp left. (If you don't want to climb the **Mezquita**, 300 metres along the road a dirt track leads to **Wp.12** and the **Mezquita** stroll).

After fifty metres the path bears right across an *acequia*. It then passes above fields of raspberries and cultivated blackberries, and goes through an overgrown section, before joining a dirt track behind a breeze-block byre, from where we can see **Busquístar**. The track descends alongside the road, crosses a stand of poplars, then joins the road which the GR7 follows all the way into **Busquístar**.

We also follow the road, but ten metres before the village limits sign and (on our left) a *no potable fuente*, we leave the GR and turn right onto a dirt path descending steeply behind a black lamppost (**Wp.8, 90M**).

The path descends into the lower part of **Busquístar** between another *no potable fuente* and a couple of concrete benches below shady plane trees. Beyond the *fuente*, we continue in the same direction down a concrete lane passing a sign for the 'Camino al Río & Ferreirola'. Descending at each junction, we pass **Las Lillas bar**, after which a final steep descent emerges between a PR waypost and (hidden round the corner) a sign for the 'Camino a Ferreirola' (**Wp.9, 100M**). We take the dirt path on the right towards **Ferreirola**.

The path descends past a goat farm (your nose will tell you!) then climbs to briefly follow an *acequia*. Just after it crosses the *acequia*, peer through the trees ahead and you should be able to pick out some stone walls nestling in a rocky outcrop: this is the **Mezquita**.

After a level section alongside another *acequia*, the path joins a new dirt track down from the road. We climb the dirt track for fifty metres then, when it bears sharp right, take the old mule trail on the left, from where we can see the path beyond the *río* climbing the **Pechos de Carriguelas** (see Walk 25).

Five minutes later, the path passes an overhanging rock and a concrete triangulation post, thirty metres after which there's a junction. Ignore the path descending on the left and take the path on the right towards **Ferreirola**.

If you don't want to climb the Mezquita
Follow this path to **Cortijo la Guarda** and return to **Atalbéitar** via Walk 24.

To climb the Mezquita
Take the Ferreirola path and, ten paces after the junction, next to an old red arrow on a rock, turn right to follow a very faint path climbing between two small holm oaks (**Wp.10, 115M**).

The path, marked by occasional red dots, is reasonably clear at first as it winds up past mini-terraces, but higher up it tends to get lost in brambles. After 4-5 minutes, about halfway up, you should find yourself faced with a red cross telling you not to climb straight ahead. In fact, though the path does bear right, it's so embrambled that you're better off ignoring the cross and going straight up to the right of the rocks for an easy scramble onto a clearer stretch of the path. Behind the cross, we bear left to traverse a slab of rock with a red line in the middle, and head towards a half-dead olive tree, shortly after which we reach the **Mezquita (Wp.11, 125M)**.

This is an exceptional site, well worth the climb, with the best views to be found anywhere in the valley. More recently, it's been used as a byre, but in Moorish times (possibly as far back as the eighth century) it was a stronghold controlling the passes over the **Sierra Mecina** that were vital to the silk trade: to the south is the **Carriguelas** pass (Walk 25), to the west the path snakes up from **Fondales** bridge (Walk 25), and to the east the **Busquístar** 'Camino al Río' (Walks 8 & 26). There's also a remarkable threshing circle built into a huge slab of rock.

To return to **Atalbéitar**, we will circle the valley dividing it from the **Mezquita**, passing the ruined mill perched on a promontory midway between the two. To start, we take the path between the buildings and the threshing circle, then cross the rock immediately below the **Mezquita (N)**.

Ducking under the skeleton of the chestnut tree directly behind the **Mezquita**, we then follow the waymarks along the ridge, climbing onto the rocks just to the left of another concrete triangulation post, and squeezing between the boulders at the highest point of the ridge (the cartographic Mezquita).

After the 'peak', litter and beer cans mark the favoured picnic spot of the agricultural labourers who work the nearby fields. The path crosses the fields within sight of the road and the avenue of trees (**Wp.7**) to join a dirt track (**Wp.12, 140M**).

Suggested Strolls

Pitres - Fuente Agria (Wps. 1-2)

Atalbéitar - the mill (Wps. 3-4 + 13)

Pórtugos - Fuente Agria (Wps. 6-7)
The **Mezquita** from the road (gr-421). Take the dirt track 300 metres after the GR7 leaves the road / 800 metres from **Pórtugos Fuente Agria** (If coming from the E, 500 metres from the *'no potable' fuente* at the western limit of **Busquístar**). Bear left at the Y-junction, take the first path on the right then follow the ridge to the **Mezquita** (**Wp.11**). Return via the main walk to the dirt track (**Wp.12**), turn right for the road.

To return to **Atalbéitar**, we turn left on the dirt track and, when the track bears left some fifty metres later, continue straight ahead onto a path between the fields. Two fields later, the path dips to the left of a small house with a pretty garden. We bear right below the garden onto a narrower, shadier stretch.

After descending past another little house, we bear right again at a junction beside a waypost (**Wp.13, 150M**) shortly before the mill. Five minutes after winding round the mill promontory, we come to the junction with the GR7 (**Wp.4**). We return to **Atalbéitar** and/or **Pitres** on the GR7.

24. TAHÁ 2

Four linked strolls between the lower villages of the **Tahá** along pleasant, peaceful, easy paths and mule trails with one slightly rougher section between **Fondales** and **Ferreirola**. **Ferreirola** is the last toponymal link with another phenomenon for which **La Tahá** is famed, the extraordinarily high iron content of its springs, which give the water such a distinctive taste (hence the **Fuentes Agrias** at **Pitres** and **Portúgos**; *agrio* meaning sour) and lends the riverbeds their startling ochre tint – some rocks literally seem to be bleeding rust. The **Tahá**'s original name was *Ferreira*. This route is ideal for a relaxing day after some of the more strenuous mountain walks. In summer, keep an eye open for the pungent white-flowered oregano. All these traditional routes between villages are peppered with slip paths into the fields. Unless otherwise stated, always stick to the main path. For simplicity's sake, I use 'path' to describe all the routes taken, though several would qualify as mule trails. Park along the road leading into **Atalbéitar**.

*Timing (Full figure of eight – 2 hours)

Atalbéitar - Ferreirola	15 mins	**Fondales - Ferreirola**	30 - 40 mins
Ferreirola - Fondales	20 - 25 mins	**Ferreirola - Atalbéitar**	35 mins

NB
Since many people will probably want to break this up into shorter strolls, waypoint timings are given between villages, not on the basis of the entire walk. You'll probably take longer than the stated time, not because you have to stop to catch your breath or because we went belting round like maniacs, but because you'll want to savour the tranquillity of the place.

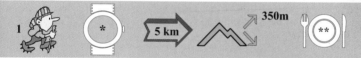

1 | * | 5 km | 350m | **

3 if anything's open, which it probably won't be, in which case 0. The **Al Jipe bar in **Mecinilla** and the hotel in **Mecina** are more reliable and are only about ten minutes away from **Fondales**.

From the first house on the western edge of **Atalbéitar** (**Wp.1, 0M**), we take the short concrete drive down towards the dark red doors and immediately bear right onto a dirt path winding down past almond groves, agave, blackberry and mulberry. After crossing an *acequia* (**Wp.2, 7M**), we bear left below a peach and plum orchard within sight of **Ferreirola** church. We then pass a long, narrow waterhut and the path broadens, bringing us into **Ferreirola** a little over ten minutes from **Atalbéitar**.

Maintaining direction into **Ferreirola**, we pass between a *lavadero* and the **Villa Kiko**. We then follow the alley descending below the church square, passing on our left the **Calle El Cerezo**, the **Villa Paquita** and **Los Monteros** before climbing slightly to reach a tiny stone cabin beside a signpost, 'GR142 Mecina-Fondales 30" (**Wp.3, 20M**). Before proceeding, it's worth peering over the cabin door to see a magnificent old clay oven.

Ferreirola – Fondales

Fifteen metres after the GR sign, the path bears left at a waypost, and winds down above an olive grove. At a Y-junction halfway along the olive grove, we take the upper path climbing past a fig tree, shortly after which we see **Fondales** ahead.

After descending over a rocky section, the path winds along the slopes through tangled blackberry bushes and dense *retama* dotted with occasional acacia, olive, chestnut and fig trees. Climbing slightly between huge rocks it crosses a concrete bridge (**Wp.4, 10M**) over the **Río Bermejo**.

A brief climb past some poplars precedes a section between an *acequia* and another olive grove before we the cross *acequia* and continue past an immense chestnut tree and a water reservoir. The path follows another *acequia* till, about fifty metres after the chestnut tree, we dip down below the *acequia* (**Wp.5, 15M**) and descend to a stream and a tiny *fuente* with benches, a few minutes from **Fondales**.

In **Fondales**, we bear left after the GR142 waypost ('Ferreirola 30'') to descend along the outskirts of the village. We keep bearing left till we pass underneath a broad *tinao* with brown garage doors on the left, immediately after which we see a GR142 sign 'Órgiva 5h30''.

Fondales – Ferreirola

We follow the GR142 concreted lane down past a *fuente/lavadero* where it turns into a dirt path. The subsequent descent is clear except for one slightly ambiguous moment where the path divides next to a pomegranate tree with a prickly pear bush behind it. We take the narrower, rougher path to the left, descending through a small poplar wood to an idyllic spot beside a Roman bridge (**Wp.6, 10M**) over the **Río Trevélez**.

Bearing left at the bridge, we leave the GR142 and follow the right bank of the **Río Trevélez**, almost immediately crossing a stream over large slabs of smooth stone. Beyond the stream, a yellow waymark indicates a rough path that zigzags up through big bushes of *retama*.

We follow this path, crossing an eroded, rocky section and climbing towards a small chestnut tree where there's a very old, very faint yellow dot on a rock, and the path becomes clearer. After winding through a small stand of chestnut, the path climbs steeply then bears right on a gentler slope below a long rocky outcrop topped with a couple of dead chestnuts.

The rocks give way to stone retaining walls until the path bears left then right to pass a partially dead chestnut, after which it winds up below an acacia to rejoin the outward route (**Wp.7, 25M**). Turning right here, we reach **Ferreirola** five minutes later, where we retrace our steps to the church square.

If you started this route from **Fondales** or the Roman bridge, you'll find the church by continuing straight on past the GR sign and bearing left after the **Villa Paquita** to climb to the *fuente/lavadero* next to the church square.

From the *fuente/lavadero*, we follow the GR waymarks in the lane below the **Villa Kiko (Calle Rosario)** across **Ferreirola** until **Calle Rosario** bears right and then left to join the path marked 'Busquístar 50''.

Ferreirola - Atalbéitar

A few minutes from **Ferreirola**, we come to the celebrated **Fuente La Gaseosa (Wp.8, 3M)**, decorated with ceramics depicting the seasons. At least a sip of its extraordinary tasting waters is obligatory. After the *fuente*, we cross the bridge over the **Barranco del Castañar** and follow a broad path above a large threshing circle before climbing to cross another bridge over the watercourse from **Pórtugos' Fuente Agria**. Fifty metres later, a third bridge leads onto an open sheet of rock, **Cortijo de la Guarda (Wp.9, 15M)**, with fine views down the **Río Trevélez**. The GR142 continues east, linking up with Walk 23.

Immediately after **Cortijo La Guarda**, we leave the GR and take the clear path on the left (**NE**) up to another junction, where we bear left again. Climbing steeply, we cross the **Fuente Agria** watercourse again, after which the gradient moderates and we come into a shady area.

After crossing an *acequia*, we follow the main path up past various branches until it emerges from the tree cover, where it swings left and climbs alongside a terracing wall to another bridge over the **Barranco del Castañar (Wp.10, 30M)**.

We cross the *barranco* and an *acequia* to climb a narrow, possibly water-logged path densely lined with brambles. Just after a sign on the left saying 'Propriedad Particular - Ganado', we bear right, away from a terrace (**Wp.11, 32M**) and climb to **Atalbéitar** fifty metres later. Turn left to cross the village and return to **Wp.1 (35M)**.

Suggested Strolls
Ferreirola - Fuente Gaseosa/Cortijo la Guarda (Wps. 8-9) GR142
Ferreirola – Río Bermejo (Wps. 3-4) GR142
Fondales - Río Bermejo (Wp.4) GR142
Fondales - Roman Bridge (Wp.6) GR142
Atalbéitar - Ferreirola (Wps. 1-3)

25. SIERRA MECINA

An easy walk (despite the extraordinary descent after **Wp.5**) using the GR142, dirt tracks and PRs, and taking in two of the Moorish silk-route passes. The views are spectacular. *Cabra montés* can occasionally be seen near **La Corona** (see map). And it's worth pausing at **Wp.6**; the bridge appears to be man-made, but in fact is built on a natural arc of rock spanning the spectacular gorge. Park in the tiny car-park at the entrance to **Fondales** or if full, a little way up the road.

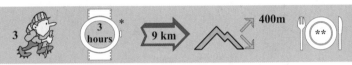

*   add 30 mins either way
          if descending from **Pitres**.
**   as per Walk 24

<table>
<tr><td colspan="2">Suggested Strolls</td></tr>
</table>

Fondales – Mecinilla Climb along the road, return via the path.

1 km west of the junction of the **Trevélez/Torviscón** roads (see Walk 8 Wp.11) take the dirt track along the **Sierra Mecina** and/or down to the **Baños de Panjuila**. The main track can be used by cars from **Wp.4** to **Wp.3** and beyond.

Start for bus users
If arriving by bus, the track from **Pitres** to **Fondales** starts on the main road opposite the **Paseo Maritimo**. Take the concrete lane to the right of **La Meta** restaurant and follow the mule trail down to **Mecina (15M)**. Bear left on the concrete lane into **Mecina**, then take either the second or third turning on the right down to the *Ayuntamiento de la Tahá* noticeboard. Bear right and follow the road round the hotel and church down to **Mecinilla (20M)**. Enter **Mecinilla** to the right of **Al Jipe** bar and follow the main alley to a *fuente* dated '1964'. Bear left, then right, then left again to join the path to **Fondales**. At the road, take the path on the right of the garage with red and white doors down to **Fondales** car-park (**Wp.,1 30M** – subsequent times from **0M**).

Start from Fondales car park
From Fondales car-park (**Wp.1, 0M**), we follow the lane into the village and take the first right next to house Number 3. We then continue descending till a lane on the left passes under a *tinao* and joins the GR142 down to **Fondales** bridge (see Walk 24).

Crossing the bridge, we follow the GR142 (**SW**) as it climbs above the river on a broad, easy path. Twenty minutes from the bridge, the path crosses a rockslide then zigzags up **El Aguadero** to join the end of a rough dirt track (**Wp.2, 45M**).

We follow the dirt track up behind a newly built house to join the main **Sierra Mecina** dirt track (**Wp.3, 55M**). Leaving the GR142, which bears right for a long, dry, dreary drag down to **Órgiva** (it's all tarmac and *retama* - if you want

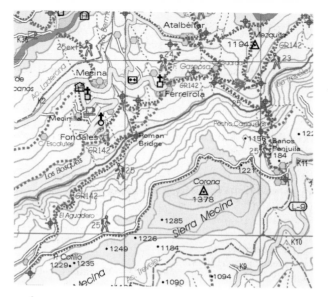

to go to **Órgiva**, get a bus), we turn left to follow the track along the **Sierra Mecina**.

The track climbs gently with fine views of the **Tahá**, the cliffs of **Carriguelas** and **Helechones**, and the old iron mines at **Cerro Conjuro**, before descending toward a group of houses just above the **Trevélez-Torviscón** road (L-9).

At the houses, just before Number 4, we take the wayposted track on the left (**Wp.4, 95M**) to descend past the ruins of the **Baños de Panjuila** (on our right and virtually imperceptible) to the cliffs of the **Pecho de las Carriguelas** or **Carihuelas** (**Wp.5, 105M**) where the track turns into a path.

If you want to picnic, there's a nice spot on the left just before the descent, among ash and poplar in a couple of tiny cliff top fields. There are also nice terraces at the bottom, on the left just before the bridge.

From the top, it's hard to believe there's a way down to the river, but in fact an easy path zigzags down causing no difficulty, even for those who suffer acute vertigo. We cross the bridge (**Wp.6, 125M**) and take the path climbing past the ruined mill.

Ignoring a branch on the right ten metres later (climbing to **La Mezquita** and **Busquístar** - see Walk 23), we stay on the main path to pass another waypost and a ruined cabin before rejoining the GR142 (**Wp.7, 135M**).

Bearing left here, we cross the rock shelf at the **Cortijo de la Guarda** (**Wp.8, 136M**) and follow the GR142 (Walk 24 in the opposite sense) across a series of watercourses to the **Fuente Agria** and **Ferreirola**. After the first *tinao*, turn right up an alley that immediately bears left and crosses Ferreirola to the *fuente/lavadero* in front of the church. Follow Walk 24 back to **Fondales**.

26.

LOS HELECHONES, EL PORTICHUELO DE CÁSTARAS & LOS CERILLOS NEGROS

A glorious, wild walk exploring a little-known, scarcely visited end of the **Tahá**, climbing to the **Cerillos Negros** firewatch hut to take in stunning views of the **Trevélez Gorge**, then descending by the easternmost 'silk-route' pass over the **Sierra Mecina**. The only drawback is that it also involves a couple of kilometres on the road. There's very little traffic though, the views from the road are excellent, and the ascent and descent out of and into the **Tahá** are so exceptional, I suspect most walkers would happily do double the distance on the road. *Helecho* means bracken or fern, not that it's much in evidence nowadays. Park in the main square in **Busquístar**.

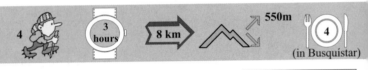

4   3 hours   8 km   550m   4
(in Busquístar)

Buses back: if you don't want to do the full circuit, the bus passes **Wp.7** at about 5.20pm

Short version
To the bridge (**Wp.5**) 50 minutes (one-way)

From the main square in **Busquístar**, we take the concrete lane to the right of the **Bar Vargas** then the first dirt track on the left, signposted 'Camino Helechal' (**Wp.1, 0M**). Sticking to the main track, we ignore all branches as it climbs gently to a threshing circle from where we can see the **Cerillos Negros** firewatch hut.

We then follow the increasingly narrow dirt track as it passes behind a two-storey concrete house and ignore all branches until we come to a cross-roads (**Wp.2, 15M**) with a new dirt track. The track we've been following continues on the far side as a narrow path that eventually leads to **Los Llanos**.

We, however, bear right on the new dirt track to pass behind a white-painted *cortijo*, beyond which a narrow path descends to a second, gated *cortijo*. Immediately after the gate, there are two paths on the right. We take the second path to pass below the pasture in front of the *cortijo* and descend (**NE**) towards the river.

Fifty metres above the river, we bear right at a Y-junction (**Wp.3, 30M**) and descend to another gate, after which the path dips and rises across the watercourses of the **Barrancos del Tesoro** and **de los Llanos** before climbing steeply to a third gate. We continue climbing to a small chestnut tree then bear right, heading upriver to pass in front of a ruin (**Wp.4, 40M**).

From the ruin, we descend to a small wood where the path is eroded by a couple of torrents. Beyond the wood, there's yet another gate, after which a gentle climb and brief descent lead to the bridge (**Wp.5, 50M**), which looks

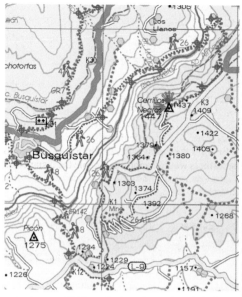

terrifying as you approach but seems solid enough once you're on it.

Beyond the bridge, a clear path climbs below the cliffs to cross a meagre watercourse next to a ruin (**Wp.6, 60M**) (visible from before the bridge) where the way up to **Portichuelo** begins.

It's worth pausing here, partly for a breather beneath the ruin's shady walnut tree, partly to enjoy the fine views back towards **Busquístar**, but also to orient yourself. If you look up from directly behind the ruin, you can see some of the concrete crash barrier along the **Trevélez** road and, to the south, the firewatch hut. Like most climbs, this one's a lot easier than it looks.

We take the path that bears right behind the ruin to re-cross the watercourse a little higher up, after which it climbs steeply, hopefully passing occasional cairns. If the cairns have been knocked down, stick to the clearer traces (most of the others are shortcuts) as they wind up to cross the broad **Acequia de Almegíjar** in a little under fifteen minutes.

Beyond the *acequia*, the increasingly broad and clear path continues climbing, meandering through some massive rocks before emerging at the junction of the **Trevélez-Juviles** & **Torviscón** roads (**Wp.7, 85M**).

Turning right, we follow the **Torviscón** road for just under 300 metres. As it comes into a slight rise, we leave the road to take a faint path on the right (**Wp.8, 90M**) climbing through the pine trees. The path soon loses definition, but if you stick to the right of the pine wood, a series of goat tracks along the ridge lead up to a little pass between two rocky outcrops where the path becomes clearer, winding along the cliff tops (near enough for gawping, far enough for comfort) before climbing gently to the firewatch tower (**Wp.9, 100M**) for exceptional views of the **Trevélez Gorge** from its headwaters all the way down to the western end of the **Tahá de Pitres**.

To descend from the firewatch hut, we take the dirt track down to the road (**Wp.10, 110M**), where we have a choice of routes to the mule trail/GR142 back to **Busquístar**. It's quicker, easier and quite as attractive to follow the road (2.3 km). However, if you're a purist and will not walk on tarmac without some overwhelming compulsion, you can take the alternative route across the old iron mines of **Cerro del Conjuro**. Be warned though: this is very rough walking, frequently off-path, and virtually indescribable! I'll do my best though.

The start is easy enough. We follow the road for a hundred metres then, as it winds into an S-bend, bear left onto the chained dirt track into the mines. After crossing the first extraction site, we bear right on a broad gravel track passing a solitary stand of holm oak. At the remains of a small concrete hut from where we can see **Busquístar**, we bear left to follow a well-trodden goat track running alongside abandoned telegraph poles till it bears right and disappears amid the scrub next to a small rocky outcrop.

To the left of this outcrop, an infinitesimal goat trail descends to a clearly visible, denuded platform, from where we can see another S-bend in the road, which is our next objective. We now descend through another area of scrub at the edge of this platform to a dirt track ten metres below, from where a succession of dirt tracks appear to wind down nicely to the road - they don't.

The first four dirt-tracks/terraces don't link up, so instead we have to maintain a westerly direction for some VERY rough walking along a series of goat tracks so faint they're virtually invisible. After the fourth terrace-track, we can follow the dirt tracks, but not all the way to the road.

Just as the dirt track comes back into view of **Busquístar**, about one hundred metres above the road and the roofless ruins of the mine works, we abandon the track and take another VERY rough 'way' (it's not a path but there are occasional stretches churned up by the goats) zigzagging down toward the ruins, just to the right of which, some steps hidden by clumps of *retama*, lead down to the lowermost track and the road.

We then follow the road for the last few hundred metres to the GR142 at the junction with the L-9 to **Cástaras**, about half-an-hour from **Wp.10**. From here it takes 30-40 minutes to return to **Busquístar**: see Walk 8 Wps. 11-13.

Suggested Strolls

Follow the start to the threshing circle for fine views up the valley.

Los Cerillos Negros. Just over 7 km from **Trevélez** bridge (dir. **Juviles**) turn right on the **Cástaras/Torviscón** road (**Wp.7**) and park 1 km later at (**Wp.10**). Follow the road BACK to **Wp.8** then follow the described walk to return to the car.

27. RÍO CULO PERRO

Yes, if you know any Spanish, it does mean what you think it means. If you don't, *culo perro* is an indelicate way of describing a dog's bottom. I don't care to delve into the toponymy of this, but despite the name it's a fine walk made exceptional if you have the pathfinding skills to link it with the lower half of Walk 28. It's especially worthwhile finding the way down in summer as returning via the shady river path is cooler than staying on the exposed path above the **Crestones de los Posteros**. If you do take the 'link' please add to the cairns. Apart from the walk through the village, the way up is nearly all gentle climbing. Due to their proximity, **Wps. 9&10** are marked by a single waypoint symbol on the map. If you intend doing the loop, park in the **Plaza de la Iglesia**. If not, park in the **Plaza Barrío Medio** and follow Walk 29 through the village. To reach the parking spots from the main square/tourist strip, take the road signposted for the *ayuntamiento* up past the Spar supermarket, until it bears round towards **Restaurante Casa Julio**. Carry straight on for the **Plaza de la Iglesia**. For the **Barrio Medio**, turn left after the restaurant and then sharp right when you come to the hostal and **Jamones Fernando**.

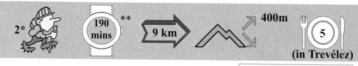

2*	190 mins **	9 km	400m	5 (in Trevélez)

* (once out of the village!)
** one way to the **Río Culo Perro** 1 hour 35 mins

Suggested Strolls

Bear left at **Wp.2** for a pleasant stroll up through pasture meadows.

From the **Plaza de la Iglesia** in **Trevélez' Barrío Bajo**, we take the aptly named **Calle Cuesta** ('Hill Street') up to a T-junction next to a *fuente* with a bench carved in the rock. We turn left here, then right fifty metres later, to climb a cobbled lane up to **Calle Carcel**. We then take the narrow concrete alley to the left of the *comidas/camas/jamones* sign, turn right on **Calle Horno**, left at the *lavadero*, then take the first path on the left (**Wp.1, 0M**).

The path, which is in fact broad enough to qualify as a mule trail, climbs steadily to a Y-junction (**Wp.2, 10M**) beside a stand of poplars, where we bear right to continue on the main trail, climbing past two *cortijos* and ignoring occasional branches into fields.

Fifty metres after the mule trail passes between a large stone *cortijo* (on the left) and a byre (on the right), we ignore the waymarked route on the left up to **Siete Lagunas** (**Wp.3, 40M**) and continue along the mule trail (**N**), which soon dwindles to a dirt path.

The path becomes stonier and drier, gradually climbing to pass a plaque (**Wp.4, 75M**) commemorating two *Guardia Civiles* killed in 1957 in a gun battle with one of the guerrilla groups that took to the mountains after the civil

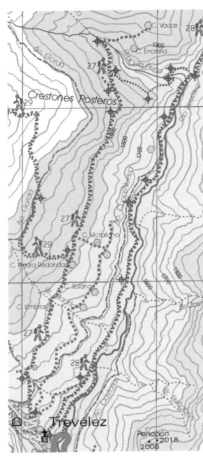

war and stayed there for the next twenty odd years.

It then winds up to cross the **Crestones de los Posteros** into the **Río Culo Perro** valley, where it gradually descends (**NW**) to a Y-junction (**Wp.5, 85M**). We take the right-hand branch descending into the valley to a faint cow path branching off to the right (**Wp.6, 88M**) marked by a large cairn, I hope – I certainly built one, anyway.

To return by the same route
If you intend returning by the same route, stay on the main path and descend to the **Río Culo Perro** (**Wp.7, 95M**) next to a rough wooden bridge, beyond which the path climbs to the **Cortijo de las Vacas**.

To link up with the Río Trevélez
To link up with the **Río Trevélez**, we take the cow path at **Wp.6**. Beware though, you need good route finding skills. What follows is a lot of detail for a very short distance, but there's only one way down that doesn't involve blundering through brambles or pitching over five metre drops, so hopefully every word is justified. Look down to the junction of the **Ríos Culo Perro** and **Trevélez**. On the left bank of the **Río Culo Perro**, there's a large, intensely green meadow. On the right bank, an escarpment climbs away from the meadow, culminating fifty metres above the river in an outcrop of rock, just to the right of which, you should be able to pick out a threshing circle. This is our first objective

From the cairn, we follow the cow path along the flank of the valley (**SE**), crossing a shallow depression, after which the path descends slightly towards a grassy platform in front of the white-fronted **Cortijo Encinilla** on the other side of the river. The cow path then heads in a more easterly direction, dividing just above the grassy platform. We can't see the threshing circle from here, but stick to the higher traces of the path as it swings back to the right (**SE**), after which the threshing circle comes into view again.

Just before it bears round onto a rocky ridge, we abandon the cow path at a point marked by a second cairn (**Wp.8, 105M** – all subsequent times exclude the time between **Wps. 6&7**) and zigzag down the scrubby/scree slope towards the threshing circle, taking care to keep above the taller scrub running up from the river. There's an old barbed-wire fence just above the threshing circle with a gate in the middle, beyond which a very faint path descends directly to the threshing circle, about five minutes from the cow path.

Bearing round to the right of the threshing circle, we come to the remains of an old cabin built into the rock. We then descend between the ruined cabin wall and another outcrop of rock (**NE**) down to a solitary holm oak and a broken barbed-wire fence above the junction of the rivers.

Crossing the barbed-wire fence, we maintain a north-easterly direction toward the river junction and another large cairn (**Wp.9, 115M**) thirty metres below the barbed-wire fence. We bear left here and follow a <u>very</u> faint trail (**NW**) until we see another cairn, still on the right bank of the **Río Culo Perro**, on a small grassy knoll below a large poplar. Don't be tempted by any previous 'shortcuts' down to the river – they all end up in brambles. The 'trail' bears right then zigzags down to the cairn (**Wp.10, 125M**).

After fording the **Río Culo** Perro (you may have to take your boots off in Spring), we descend through the meadow seen from **Wp.6**, passing in front of a semi-abandoned *cortijo* and crossing a marshy dell to a ford over the **Río Trevélez** fifteen metres upriver.

After the ford, a rough gate in a barbed-wire fence (**Wp.11, 130M**) leads onto a heavily water-logged path (you might be forgiven for thinking you were walking <u>in</u> the river rather than alongside it) and a ten minute descent to a bridge over the river, just next to the source of the **Acequia Nueva**.

We cross the *acequia* twice and, fifty metres after the second crossing, bear left, away from the *acequia* and back towards the river. We then stay on the right bank of the river all the way to **Trevélez**. It may sometimes be flooded, especially in spring, but don't be beguiled onto the left bank by apparently drier routes: they all end in deep fords with swift currents. (See Walk 28 WPs 7-1 for details.) It takes about one hour to reach **Trevélez** from **Wp.11**.

28. Headwaters of the RÍO TREVÉLEZ via the CAMINO DE GRANADA

A straightforward walk, following the **Río Trevélez** from the domestic landscape near the village up to the wilder area below **El Horcajo**, a traditional pasture where, according to Gerald Brenan, shepherds were once wont to set upon unwary travellers and relieve them of anything relievable. Fortunately, times have changed but the landscape remains the same. The only drawback is that, even though the river may be dry in summer between **Wps. 3&6**, much of the path is often flooded; not enough to impede progress, but sufficient to qualify as a river itself anywhere else. Take a towel; there are fine plunge-pools throughout, though beware of slippery rocks. Park in the **Plaza de la Iglesia** (see Walk 27).

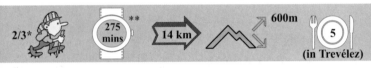

2/3* | 275 mins** | 14 km | 600m | 5 (in Trevélez)

* 2 to **Hoya del Chordí**
  3 to the headwaters
** 2 hours 35 mins up, 2 hours down

(Also see map for Walk 27.)

From the **Plaza de la Iglesia** in **Trevélez' Barrío Bajo**, we take the **Calle Cuesta** and turn right immediately behind the church (**Wp.1, 0M**) onto the broad dirt track down to the river. One hundred metres after the track crosses a watercourse, we bear left onto a narrow dirt path (**Wp.2, 5M**) that descends to the river twenty minutes later.

Bearing left at a Y-junction (**Wp.3, 30M**), we climb briefly before rejoining the river above a series of small, improvised dams. After fording a shallow affluent (**Wp.4, 40M**) and splashing along a section resembling an *acequia* (**Wp.5, 45M**) (it _is_ still the path), we bear right on a bank of raised earth by-passing a meadow.

The path then climbs briefly to follow the **Acequia Nueva** before crossing a rough bridge (**Wp.6, 55M**) shortly after which we have to cross the *acequia* again and take a larger bridge onto the river's left bank. For the second crossing of the *acequia*, there's usually a couple of logs lying around to fashion a makeshift ford or bridge, but if they've disappeared and you don't have long legs, you may have to take your boots off and wade across.

We then climb the left bank of the river, passing the

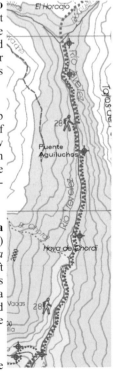

ford (**Wp.7, 70M**) just above the junction of the **Ríos Trevélez** and **Culo Perro** (see Walk 27), shortly after which another deep *acequia* crossing marks the start of the more substantial climb towards the **Hoya del Chordí** (identifiable by a *cortijo* on the right bank), where the mountains become wilder and rockier. Sticking to the left bank and ignoring all branches away from the river, we descend into the **Hoya del Chordí** along a water-logged path.

The path loses definition in a meadow beneath a large shady ash with a cow's skull hanging halfway up its trunk (**Wp.8, 100M**), but maintaining direction we soon pick up a badly eroded rock-laid stretch running alongside the river below the meadow. After splashing through another flooded stretch, we cross another small *acequia* and descend on a drier stretch to the river below the **Tajos de Peña Cabrera**.

Suggested Strolls

Río Trevélez – an easy stroll though the river stretch requires some acrobatic leaping about and ducking and weaving! From the **Plaza de la Iglesia**, take **Calle Cuesta**, turning right immediately behind the church onto a concrete lane and, thirty metres later, left onto a grassy path. Bear left at the white house and follow the path till it joins the dirt track down to the bridge over the river.

Cross the bridge and take the narrow path down the left bank of the river. Leave the path when it climbs away from the river and follow the river all the way to the main road bridge, sometimes on the left bank, sometimes on the right bank, sometimes actually in the river hopping from rock to rock! NB this second stretch is only for summer; otherwise it will probably be impassable; you will in any case get your feet wet. Just south of the road bridge, a small dam forms a swimming pool in summer.

From here, if you look up towards the **Horcajo** at the end of the valley, you can see a small white building, which is about a hundred metres above our destination. The path continues along alternately dry and waterlogged sections till it crosses a very rudimentary wood and slate bridge (**Puente de los Aguiluchos, Wp.9, 125M**) and, five minutes later, crosses back onto the left bank by a smaller slightly sturdier bridge.

After the second bridge, a succession of steady climbs leads up to the junction of the **Ríos Juntillas** and **Puerto de Jeres** that form the **Río Trevélez**. En route, there's a junction of paths marked with cairns (**Wp.10, 150M**). We ignore the path on the right (the way to **Jeres de Marquesado**) and bear left on the main path to reach the junction of the rivers five minutes later (**Wp.11, 155M**). We return by the same route.

29. SIETE LAGUNAS + optional descent via MIRADOR DE TREVÉLEZ

Bit of a marathon this one, but amply rewarded by a real sense of wilderness above **Campiñuela** and access to one the Alpujarras' most celebrated sites, the **Seven Lagoons**. Needless to say, the views are stunning throughout. So's the climbing! The upper reaches of the **Río Culo Perro (Wp.5)** are worth visiting even if you don't do the final climb to the lagoons. And if you're really feeling lazy, you can join one of the horse-riding excursions up to **Las Chorreras** and walk to the lagoons from there (contact *Rutas a Caballo* in Trevélez' Barrío Alto 958 858 601). The path is clear, except briefly after **Wp.4** & between **Wps.7-9**. The descent from the **Mirador de Trevélez**, is an attractive route that also links the **Poqueira** and **Trevélez** gorges, but don't do it in reverse. The ingredients of a stimulating if knee-breaking descent would be dreary misery as a climb. The clear path from **Wp.7** is another classic ascent of the **Mulhacén** that takes around three hours.

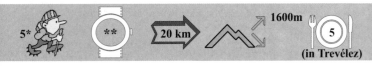

5*   **   20 km   1600m   5 (in Trevélez)

* though not so long, this is every bit as tough as Walk 21 and climbs even further (1600 metres). If you think that sounds rough, you may like to bear in mind that every August there's a race [this is not a joke] from **Trevélez** to the **Mulhacén**, a 2000 metre climb; last year the quickest lunatics did it in under 3 hours!	**Short Version** To the headwaters of the **Río Culo Perro (Wp.4/5)** 3 hours 15 minutes (195M) (one-way).

** full circuit: 7 hours 10 mins (given the distance and climbing involved, allow 10 hours)

    Laguna Hondera: 3 hours 35 mins (one-way) (likewise, allow 5 hours)

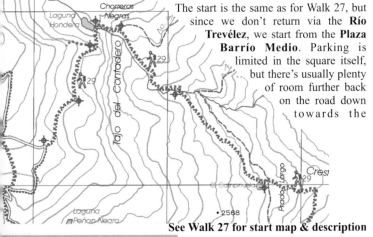

The start is the same as for Walk 27, but since we don't return via the **Río Trevélez**, we start from the **Plaza Barrío Medio**. Parking is limited in the square itself, but there's usually plenty of room further back on the road down towards the

See Walk 27 for start map & description

Barrío Bajo.

Taking the narrow street past the excellent **Panadería Federico**, we turn left at the *comidas/camas/jamones* sign, right on **Calle Horno**, left at the *lavadero*, then take the first path on the left (**Wp.1, 0M**). We then follow Walk 27 to **Wp.3 (40M)** and bear left at the 'Campiñuela/7 Lagunas' signpost to climb a clear path marked with cairns, wayposts and red/green waymarks.

We climb steadily for fifteen minutes, crossing two gated fences, then follow the path as it bears north, going through another gate and crossing a marshy area before climbing to the **Acequia Gorda** (**Wp.2, 85M**). We follow the *acequia* for 150 metres then bear left at a waypost to climb steadily through recently planted pine to the scattering of rocks and boulders at **Los Posteros**.

Bearing right at the upper limit of **Los Posteros**, we cross another replanted area, then bear left to climb steadily up **Prado Largo**, gradually coming in sight of the **Lomas de Mulhacén** and **Alcazaba**, and the **Chorreras Negras** waterfall feeding the **Río Culo Perro**. We then bear right above **Prado Largo** for a gentler climb to the small cabin and large threshing circle at **Cortijo de la Campiñuela (Wp.3, 135M)**, frequently misplaced on maps.

The path continues past the ruined walls of the **Campiñuela** byre (**NW**), crossing a tiny rivulet above a small reservoir. It then climbs (at first steadily then more gently) to cross a narrow torrent, after which another steady climb leads to the **Río Culo Perro** just above a narrow dike (**Wp.4, 165M**), sometimes called **El Vertedero**.

We can either follow the path till it crosses the river fifty metres later or (as mapped) cross the dyke and head upriver toward the **Tajo del Contadero** cliffs to pick up a fainter stony path climbing away from the river toward the **Chorreras**. We then follow the cairns up to a minor affluent of the **Culo Perro (Wp.5, 195M)** where a climb that has so far been at the upper limit of 'steady' suddenly turns 'steep' – and nasty! But don't be discouraged; it's tough, but not as tough as it looks.

Crossing the affluent, we climb alongside the cascade, looking out for the cairns where the path disappears under rockfalls, and soon (certainly sooner than seems possible from **Wp.5**) come to **Laguna Hondera (Wp.6, 215M)**, the largest and, despite what some maps claim, lowest of the seven lagoons tucked into the glaciation cirque defined by the **Lomas de Mulhacén** and **Alcazaba**.

We can either return by the same route or, if you can face climbing another 200

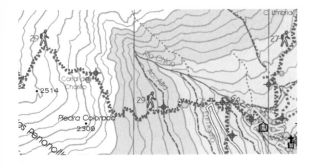

metres, make a loop via the **Loma de Mulhacén** and the **Mirador de Trevélez**.

Loma de Mulhacén and Mirador de Trevélez loop

On the **SE** tip of the ridge round the cirque, there's a tall thin cairn. At first glance there's no way up to this, but in fact to the **SE** of the **Laguna Hondera**, behind a large rock and a small windbreak (commonly known, a tad rosily to my mind, as the **Refugio Natural de Siete Lagunas**), a very faint 'way' that gradually becomes something approximating a path, does wind up past the tall thin cairn to another fatter cairn built on a large rock (**Wp.7, 225M**).

Ignoring the clear path climbing to the right along the **Cuesta** or **Cuerda de Resuello**, we head south-west from the fat cairn to cross the first of two shallow depressions or *hoyas* that lead to the **Llanos del Mulhacén**. There's neither path nor cairns to begin with, so you'll have to take my word for this, but after a couple of hundred metres you'll come to the first of a series of cairns marking the way and a slightly clearer path. You'll also probably see plenty of *cabras montés*.

Bear right as you cross this first *hoya*, staying near its upper/western limit to traverse the higher patches of grass just below the shallow cliffs, where you should find the first cairns. Maintaining a south-westerly direction, we cross a broad grassy stretch on the far side of the *hoya* to pass two cairns marking a reasonably clear trail which climbs slightly before bearing left up to a large cone-shaped cairn. The path virtually disappears again here, but faint traces and a series of tall cairns indicate the way out of the first *hoya* onto a ridge overlooking the second shallower and stonier *hoya* (**Wp.8, 245M**).

The stones are smaller here, so the trodden way is slightly clearer, and is also well marked with cairns. Again we circle round the head of the *hoya*, climbing gently to its highest recess, where a steeper path, just discernible from **Wp.8**, climbs out of the *hoya* in a **SSE** direction onto a scree slope where it disappears. We bear right here and follow the cairns off-path (**W**) as the slope gradually levels out and leads up to the **Mulhacén** branch of the **Carretera de Veleta** (**Wp.9, 260M**). We then follow this track (see Walk 21 for a generic description) to the **Mirador de Trevélez** (Walk 21 Wp.17).

Bearing left at a waypost marking the *mirador*, we leave the *carretera* to cross bare ground to another waypost at the top of the path (**Wp.10, 320M**) down to

Trevélez (visible below). We then follow this path, ignoring both the tracks over the rocky ridge to the south (the **Loma de los Penoncillos**) AND, if you care for your knees, the various shortcuts (a 1300 metre descent in 3km really doesn't need shortcuts, as well).

The path is well wayposted, passing the abandoned *cortijo* and threshing circle of the **Corral del Chorillo (Wp.11, 370M)**, and crossing first an *acequia* (**Wp.12, 400M**) then, a hundred metres below, a dirt track. It then descends to a ruin (currently being rebuilt), below which it crosses private land, passing three gates before emerging on another dirt track at a bend above two threshing circles. We take the wayposted path between the threshing circles for a final descent to the GR7 (**Wp.13, 425M**) five minutes from **Trevélez' Barrío Alto**.

30.

TREVÉLEZ - PEÑABÓN + optional descent to BÉRCHULES

'**Peñabón**' or '**Peña de los Papos**' (depending on the map) is the mammoth lump of rock looming over **Trevélez**. This route tackles the higher of the two **Peñabón** peaks (2536 metres), from where you have superb views in all directions. The **Cortijo de las Rosas (Wp.6)** is a good spot for bird watchers: we saw dozens of brilliantly coloured wasp-catchers gliding, spinning and diving above the rocks. Other walkers have reported seeing golden eagles from the peak.

The optional descent to **Bérchules** is an easy if somewhat monotonous route mainly along dirt tracks. It provides an alternative to the GR7 for linking villages and might also be useful for those staying in **Bérchules**, taking the morning bus to **Trevélez** and returning to **Bérchules** on foot. You'd have to be an early riser though - the morning bus leaves at 5.05am! Note, as a descent it is tolerable, but don't do it in reverse. It's a long drag up and the combination of climbing and monotony may well prove fatal. If you want to return to **Trevélez** from **Bérchules**, remember the evening bus also leaves at five. If you miss the bus, 'Barbero' provides a taxi service. Ask in the new houses on the right after the *fuente* as you descend toward the main road (gr-421).

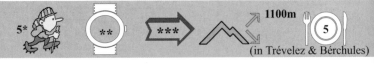

5*   **   ***   1100m   5

(in Trevélez & Bérchules)

*   The walking is easy, but you do climb 1100 metres in a little over 4 km and this is one of those Russian doll walks where you keep thinking you're there only to find yet another gruelling climb lurking behind the last one.

**   **Trevélez-Peñabón** - 3 hours (one way)
      Peñabón-Bérchules - 2 hours 15 mins (one way)

***   **Trevélez-Peñabón** - 4.3 km (one way) **Peñabón-Bérchules** - 7 km

Buses back: **Bérchules - Trevélez** 5.05 p.m.
                 Trevélez - Bérchules 3.15 p.m. / 8.30 p.m.

From **Trevélez**, we follow the GR7/Walk 5 to the **Acequia de Cástaras (Wp.2, 10M)**, where we bear right. After 150 metres, we leave the GR7 to take a clear path (green-white waymarks) climbing to the left (**Wp.3, 15M**), bearing right at the Y-junction immediately afterwards. As the path approaches a large outcrop of rock, beyond which there's a deep, dry gully, you should be able to pick out two small aerials tucked behind rocks and a couple of pine trees on the far side of the gully.

The aerials disappear briefly as the path bears left to climb alongside the gully, passing below the retaining wall of a shallow reservoir, now silted up and grassed over. Just above this reservoir (**Wp.4, 20M**), we leave the main path as it crosses the gully towards the aerials, making sure to stay on the northern side of the gully, bearing left to cross a rock slope and climb past a series of cairns towards another outcrop of rock.

Just below the outcrop of rock, the 'path' (which is virtually invisible on the rock slope) crosses the remains of an old wire gate then becomes clearer as it winds up through the rocks. It then crosses the gully (**Wp.5, 26M**) between a couple of eglantine bushes before climbing steadily (**S**), eventually winding into a pinewood a couple of hundred metres above the aerials.

The path emerges from the wood very briefly then continues climbing between the trees along a route that is sometimes faint but always well-marked with cairns, finally coming out at the wood's western limit (**Wp.6, 45M**) within sight of the white **Cortijo de las Rosas**. We bear right along the upper limit of the wood to a small rocky platform above the **Barranco de los Castaños** then turn left to climb towards the *cortijo* along a faint path marked by occasional cairns.

Leaving the *cortijo* on our left, we follow the path along the fence up to a small reservoir, beyond which another pinewood begins. We take the faint path climbing north-east between the pinewood and the **Barranco de los Castaños**. When the path splinters into a series of goat tracks, we maintain direction and climb steadily, following the main traces as they approach the pinewood again a few minutes later. We stay just to the right of the pinewood until we reach a Y-junction near their upper limit (**Wp.7, 90M**) where we bear left.

A hundred metres later, at the pinewood's westernmost tip, we turn right as the path zigzags up to the ruined **Cortijo de Prados Altos** (**Wp.8, 100M**). After the ruin, the path occasionally loses definition, so keep your eye open for cairns and stick to the main traces as they wind up to a weedy reservoir (**Wp.9, 120M**) near the head of the *barranco*.

After crossing a fence beyond the reservoir, we leave the main path as it bears south and climb alongside the watershed through the last stand of pine. When the path disappears, we head north-east, away from

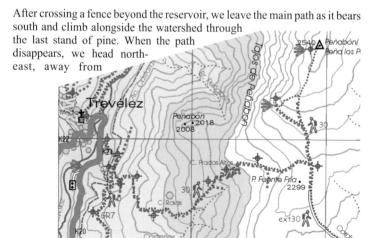

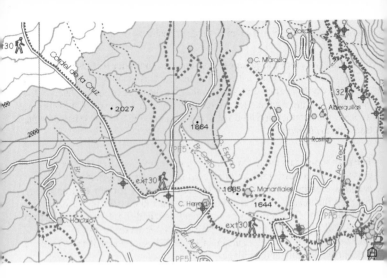

watershed, and follow the cairns through the remaining pine and scrub up to the flat ridge above **Fuente Fría** where we join the traces of an old dirt track (**Wp.10, 140M**).

We follow the dirt track north, ignoring a branch to the left (our return route), until it gradually gets fainter and finally disappears altogether. We then continue climbing across scrub and scree to pick up a clear path leading behind the first outcrop of rocks, after which we follow the ridge past two more outcrops until we reach the tall triangulation post marking the **Peñabón/Peña de los Papos** peak (**Wp.11, 180M**) where there's a tiny but sturdy and very welcome windbreak.

For a slightly different route back to **Wp.10**, we stay on the path after the first outcrop of rocks and, when it disappears, continue **SW** to join the left-hand branch of the track along the ridge which leads to a small pen (**Wp.12, 195M**) for capturing *cabra montés*, behind which there are fine views across the **Tajos del Peñabón**. We then follow the dirt track back to **Wp.10**, from where we can either return to **Trevélez** by the same route or descend to **Bérchules** via the **Cordel de la Cruz de Bérchules**.

To descend to Bérchules
For **Bérchules**, we follow the dirt track (**S**) over a small hump, after which it dips down, running into a clear logging track alongside a firebreak. After a monotonous but easy descent (easy on everything but the knees), the logging track merges with the track for the **Cortijo El Horcajo** (**Wp.13, 240M**), a potential way down to **Juviles** but unfortunately a 'permanent firing range'!

We bear left as the logging track, now better stabilised and less steep, leaves the firebreak and cuts through a pine forest, passing an open stretch above beehives before crossing more pine forest and joining PF5 (**Wp.14, 250M**). We follow PF5 to the right for 500 metres and, just after the **Cortijo de Hoya Herrera**, bear left onto a rough dirt track (**Wp.15, 260M**) descending past another pinewood towards several stands of beehives.

Immediately before the junction with another smoother dirt track (**Wp.16, 275M**), we take the shortcut path on the left to join the track lower down above the dry **Barranco de Cairo**. Following the track round the head of the *barranco*, we turn right at the Y-junction. Just after a large inhabited *cortijo*, we leave the dirt track and take a narrow dirt path (**Wp.17, 285M**) between the track and the *barranco*.

The path soon bears away from the *barranco* above a cherry orchard, before crossing another dirt track and descending towards a chestnut wood and an *acequia*. Bearing left, we follow the *acequia* path for ten metres before crossing the *acequia* and descending through more chestnut trees towards **Bérchules**, the first glimpses of which are visible through the trees. A steep descent along an old mule trail between fields leads to the outskirts of **Bérchules** next to a small *fuente* (**Wp.18, 305M**) after which it's a ten minute descent to the centre of the village.

+----------------------------------+
| **Short Version** |
| |
| It's worth climbing to |
| **Wp.6** below the |
| **Cortijo de las Rosas** |
| for the views. |
+----------------------------------+

31. CERRO MACILLA - CÁSTARAS

The **Barranco de Fuente Medina** is an enchanting little valley, leading down to the pretty village of **Cástaras**. Better still, nobody seems to know about it and the paths are all but deserted, unused except by the occasional shepherd and, if the spoors are anything to go by, the odd wild boar. However, being off the beaten track does have its drawbacks. Many paths dwindle into nothing while others have become so embrambled they're impassable. If you go exploring, be prepared to turn back. **Wps. 8, 10, 12 & 14** are not on the map.

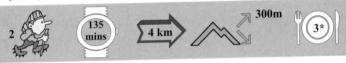

| 2 | 135 mins | 4 km | | 300m | 3* |

*   in **Cástaras** with luck, though the main **Bar Maria** is also mainly shut

To reach the start of the walk, take the dirt track (watch out for the erosion channels) on the left 1.3 km from the western limit of **Juviles**. After 600 metres, park on the flat ground between the rocks of **Cerro Macilla** and the almond groves (**Wp.1, 0M**).

On the western edge of the parking area, we take the old *acequia* path to the left of the almond grove. We follow this path as it bears left through *retama* before descending into the **Barranco de Fuente Medina**, where we bear right at a Y-junction (**Wp.2, 5M**) just before the stream to cross both the stream and, five metres later, an old *acequia*.

After passing a large abandoned reservoir, the path continues alongside a series of terraces, gradually descending to re-cross the *acequia* and veer back toward the poplar lined stream. Ignoring a branch on the right (**Wp.3, 10M**), we carry straight on, squeezing through a tunnel of *retama* to join a partially rock-laid path, crossing back onto the left bank of the now dry watercourse (**Wp.4, 15M**) amid a stand of poplars.

A clearer path marked by a white cross (not a waymark) follows the left bank down to a more densely wooded stretch of young poplars where the water re-emerges from an underground source. We continue descending, crossing another *acequia* before re-crossing the stream next to a small waterfall (**Wp.5, 30M**).

After a brief climb along the right bank, the path passes a series of clear grassy terraces before returning to the riverbed beside a large reservoir, a little way below which the three spouts of the **Fuente Solís (Wp.6, 40M)** nestle below a large overhanging rock.

We continue along the right bank on a more closely cobbled stretch which soon goes to the right of a large, partially ruined house (currently being restored), before descending to join the main track from the house down past a white water hut with a blue door to a T-junction (**Wp.7, 50M**).

If coming from Cástaras
Wp.7 can be recognised by a line of six olive trees overhanging the path and, behind them, the brick lip of a circular reservoir; there's also a small wooden sign saying 'Los Vigilantes'.

To continue to the village
We turn left and descend a concreted alley-cum-track joining the road (**Wp.8, 60M**) just west of **Cástaras**.
NB
If you're starting from **Cástaras**, this track is the one just before the '40km for 1.5km' speed limit sign.

If you don't wish to visit the village
Turn right at **Wp.7** for a steady climb to a ruin and junction of paths (**Wp.9, 73M**) on the edge of what appears to be a discrete hamlet, but is in fact the largely abandoned **Barrio Alto de Cástaras**.

After taking the left-hand branch into the 'hamlet', we bear right on the path climbing behind the first house to a broader cobbled track next to a *fuente* (**Wp.10, 75M**) where the real climb into the **Barranco de Alberquilla** begins.

Ignoring a branch on the left (**Wp.11, 77M**), we continue climbing toward the poplar topped rocks behind the hamlet, where there's a small *cortijo* with breeze block outbuildings (**Wp.12, 84M**) and, behind it, a small *acequia*.

We follow the *acequia*, ignoring a branch up to a manmade waterfall, and climb steadily to the head of the *barranco* where there's a large reservoir (**Wp.13, 90M**). Ignoring the main trail climbing to the left, we take the path bearing right behind the reservoir.

After a brief climb, the path levels out before bearing left to a small col above an almond grove, from which a mule trail zigzags back into the **Barranco de Fuente Medina**, rejoining the outward route (**Wp.14, 105M**) about thirty minutes below **Cerro Macilla**.

> **Suggested Strolls**
> Cástaras – **Barrancos de Alberquilla & Fuente Solis** (Wps.8-14 & 6-8)

32. BÉRCHULES JUNTA DE LOS RÍOS + extension to HOYA DEL BORREGO

An outstanding walk, following an exceptionally pretty *acequia* and returning along a mule trail with splendid views of the valley. There's one stretch of the *acequia* along a narrow wall above a small drop and another traversing a badly eroded slope, but otherwise the walking is easy. If your vertigo is really acute, you may wish to skip the *acequia* and take the return route both ways (see **Wp.10**). The extension, an attractive walk in its own right, is specially recommended if you want to do Walk 33. The alternative route back from the extension requires slightly better path finding skills. **Wp.5** is not marked on the map. Park in the main car-park next to the track down to the **Fuente Agria de Bérchules**.

| 3 | * | 6 km | 470m *** | 5 (in Bérchules) |

* to the **Junta de los Ríos** & back 2 hours 5 mins
for the extension add 1 hour 40 minutes (incl. return)

** 6 km + 4 km for the extension
*** 470 metres with extension, 200 metres without

Suggested Strolls

Acequia Nueva. Bear right at **Wp.2** (the main junction after the large chestnut tree, not the minor junction next to the telegraph poles) descend to the *acequia* and follow it back to a little bridge onto the horseshoe threshing circle, from where we can rejoin the main path back into **Bérchules**.

From the **Bar Los Vergeles** in **Bérchules** church square, we take **Calle Iglesia (N)**. We then cross **Plaza Arastos** and follow **Calle Real** to a triple-junction, where we continue straight ahead on **Calle García**, bearing right twenty metres later onto a concrete lane up to a *fuente/lavadero* and a broad dirt path signposted for the **Junta de los Ríos (Wp.1 0M)**.

The path runs alongside apple and pear orchards, crossing a watercourse just above a roofless mill before climbing behind a large horseshoe-shaped threshing circle, from where the **Loma de Enmedio** above the **Ríos Chico** and **Grande** is visible. After passing a second threshing circle, the old path is engulfed by a new dirt track.

Ignoring a branch on the right fifty metres after the second threshing circle (**Wp.2, 10M**), we bear left to follow the main track. Immediately after an access track into another orchard, we leave the new dirt track, and bear right to rejoin the old path (**Wp.3, 13M**) above a small reservoir protected by a sloping wire fence supported by corroded metal posts. Five metres after the flat-roofed house abutting onto the reservoir, we bear right again to join the path along the **Acequia Nueva**.

The *acequia* is a delight, flanked by chestnut, walnut, mulberry, blackberry, clover and mint, and lined with clumps of a curious pink weed. Despite occasionally going underground and passing stretches lined or walled with PVC, corrugated-iron and sheet-metal, it maintains its charm. We now follow the *acequero*'s path all the way to the **Junta de los Ríos**.

Note:

a. After a brief stretch where the water is piped underground, the path bears left and climbs slightly to run along a narrow wall for ten metres above a 3 metre drop.

b. After passing a couple of bedstead gates, a branch to the right (**Wp.4, 35M**) leads onto a natural *mirador*.

c. After the landscape becomes more barren, there's a slightly tricky stretch (**Wp.5, 60M**) where the water is piped underground and we have to scramble along an eroded slope.

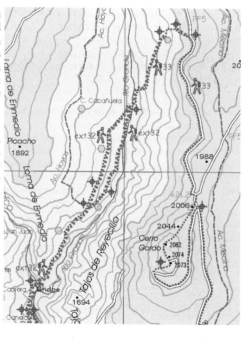

Almost immediately after **Wp.5**, another path comes in from the left (**Wp.6**). This is the return route. For now, we bear right and continue along the *acequia* for 5' to the **Junta de los Ríos**, where we cross the **Río Chico** bridge and reach the **Fábrica de Moros** ruins below the **Tajos de Reyecillo** or **Reyezuelo**, last refuge of the leaders of the 1568 Moorish rebellion (**65M**).

For the extension

We take the broad mule-track climbing to the left of the **Fábrica de Moros** ruins. A succession of three easy climbs with fine views of the **Tajos de Reyecillo** (you may spot a sizeable herd of wild boar with their babies here in spring) leads to a Y-junction (**Wp.7, 30M**).

Bearing right onto a narrower path, we pass two *cortijos*, the first inhabited in the summer, the second ruined and facing three other roofless ruins on the eastern side of the river. The path gradually descends to the river, getting narrower and more overgrown, and passing several muddy stretches, before fording the **Río Grande (Wp.8, 50M)** into a large stand of poplars, visible since the ruined *cortijo*.

For an alternative return to the Junta de los Ríos,
We hop over the rough barbed-wire fence ten metres before the ford and cross the meadow down to the river. We then follow the cow paths for the next fifteen minutes, crossing and re-crossing the river, aiming first for two large bushy poplars, then for a stone hut on a promontory on the left bank above the river (the lower of the three ruins mentioned above).

Just before the promontory, we bear right to cross the river yet again and pick up a more clearly traced cow path that almost immediately re-crosses the river! Ignoring the branch climbing to the right (my apologies, but the logic of a cow is a sorry thing) we cross back onto the right bank to follow the path as it climbs above the river (**S**).

Ignoring another minor branch after fifteen metres, we stick to the main traces, climbing gently to cross the eroded flank of a field. We then bear left at a Y-junction and pass behind the ruins of a small byre (**Wp.9, 80M**) where the path disappears. Maintaining altitude, we continue **SW** towards a stretch of fencing and two small, half-dead walnut trees, thirty metres after which we rejoin the main mule track (**85M**) fifteen minutes from the **Junta de los Ríos**.

From the **Junta de los Ríos**, it's five minutes down to the junction of paths at **Wp.6**. Crossing the watercourse feeding into the **Acequia Nueva**, we follow the path up to a *cortijo*/threshing circle, where it broadens to a mule track, following the contours of the mountain to emerge on a branch of the new dirt track (**Wp.10, 40M** from the **Junta de los Ríos**) which we join one hundred metres later. We bear left and follow the dirt track back to **Wp.3** to arrive back in **Bérchules** one hour from the **Junta de los Ríos**.

33. CERRO GORDO

A simple if slightly tame ascent, but the views on the way up are good and, from the top, excellent, while the descent along the **Río Grande** and the **Acequia Nueva** (Walk 32) is one of the most attractive routes in the region. Park as per Walk 32.

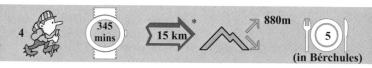

| 4 | 345 mins | 15 km | * | 880m | 5 (in Bérchules) |

*   full circuit

> **Suggested Strolls**
>
> See Pista Forestal 5

From **Bérchules** church (**Wp.1, 0M**) follow GR7/Walk 7 Wps. 8-11 to the dirt track (**Wp.2, 60M**). NOTE: the rocky outcrop visible above the **Cortijos Cortes** and **Montero** on the far side of the river, is the **Cima de Tejar** (**Wp.5**).

Turning left on the dirt track, we pass a puzzling GR7 waypost (according to the maps, it shouldn't be there!) and follow the track till it bears right at the **Cortijo Montero**. We can stay on the dirt track here, but it's quicker to go behind the **Montero** chapel and climb the slope (**E**) directly behind the *cortijo* (**Wp.3, 75M**) to rejoin the track one hundred metres later.

We then follow the dirt track above a huge concrete reservoir and, 250 metres after a U-bend, bear right on a very rough, very steep maintenance track (**Wp.4, 90M**) up to the fence below the **Tejar** pinewood. We follow this track (**N**) alongside the fence to join another track, where we turn right, cross the fence and climb (**E**) to the wide firebreak (**Wp.5, 110M**) behind the **Cima de Tejar**. To the north, you might be able to pick out the flash of a white flag beside **Cerro Gordo** firewatch hut and, to the south, on a clear day, Africa.

From the **Cima de Tejar**, we take the dirt track up the firebreak (**N**). After passing a first branch on the left twenty minutes later, the track gradually levels out before a second branch on the left (**Wp.6, 150M**) climbs to **Cerro Gordo**. We can either follow the dirt track all the way to the top or, when it turns sharp right and we see the **Mulhacén** and **Alcazaba** to the west, climb off-path directly to the firewatch hut (**Wp.7, 170M**).

From the firewatch hut, we follow a faint logging track (**N**) until it peters out on a grassy platform above the **Cerro Gordo** crags.
NB From here it's worthwhile tracing an imaginary line down from the white-walled reservoir on the eastern side of the valley to pinpoint the stand of poplars at **Wp.12**.

Staying to the right of the crags, we descend off-path, picking our way through gorse, thyme and broom, occasionally following brief stretches of goat track to join Pista Forestal 5 (**Wp.8, 185M**) at the junction with the firebreak track, fifty metres from **Wp.6**.

We turn left here and follow PF5, passing on our right two craggy outcrops overlooking a broad *barranco* leading down to two ruined *cortijos* divided by a large pasture. Seventy-five metres after a meagre spring beside a stone wall with '*Coto Privado*' daubed on it in large white letters and topped with a '*Parque Nacional*' sign, we turn left at a large cairn (**Wp.9, 215M**) to take the very faint remains of an ancient cow path (so faint and ancient it is, to all intents and purposes, 'off-path') zigzagging down to the first ruin.

The 'path' winds down twenty metres, then bears right and descends to a watercourse. We follow the left bank of the watercourse down to a slightly damp stretch then cross onto the northern side, where an irrigation canal channelled with slates marks the top of a shaley slope (**Wp.10, 220M**) descending to the first ruin. We follow a very faint 'path' across the slope then bear left for a rough, steep descent to a clear path just above the ruin (**Wp.11, 25M**).

A reasonably clear path in front of the ruin's threshing circle, recrosses the watercourse then bears away from it and gradually descends through an oak forest (**SSW**). When the path emerges from the forest, we bear right across a small field then follow the river for 150 metres to the large stand of poplars (**Wp.12, 245M**), halfway along which a ford crosses the river (Walk 32 Wp.8).

From here, we can either take the alternative descent described in Walk 32, or stay on the principal path for a gentle climb to the main mule trail (**Wp.13, 265M**) down to the **Junta de los Ríos** (**Wp.14, 285M**).

After crossing the bridge over the **Río Chico** we follow the **Acequia Nueva** for a couple of hundred metres to a path climbing off to the right (Walk 32 Wp.6), where we again have a choice of routes, either following Walk 32 down to **Bérchules** or, recommended, bearing left to continue along the *acequia* (see Walk 32 for a generic description) until it joins the new dirt track (Walk 32 Wp.3) above **Bérchules**.

When the dirt track comes to a fence next to a threshing circle, we bear right on a narrow path leading into **Bérchules** (one hour from **Wp.14**) at the top of **Calle Garcia** which leads to **Calle Real** and Plaza **Arastos**.

PRA111 MECINA-BOMBARÓN, ACEQUIA DE LOS CASTAÑOS

A gentle, domestic walk, ideal for relaxing after the rigours of the high-mountains. The route follows the **Acequia de los Castaños**, which is perhaps not the prettiest of *acequias*, most of it having been lined with concrete or even piped and interred; but the path itself is exceptional, winding through the finest chestnut wood in the Alpujarras (quite sublime when the leaves are turning in late autumn). The itinerary is a version of a 'PR'. Unfortunately, this particular PR (the A111) is so eccentrically waymarked (nothing where you need it, everything where you don't) the waymarks are rarely useful.

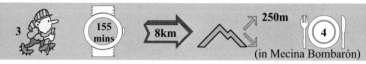

3 | 155 mins | 8km | 250m | 4
(in Mecina Bombarón)

To reach the start of the walk, take the concrete track from the western limit of **Mecina-Bombarón** (signposted 'Taller Madera Artesania') up to **Calle de Plaza Vieja** and park in the **Plaza Vieja** itself. From the **Plaza Vieja**, take the small street climbing beside the *fuente* (signposted 'Bérchules 2h') and bear right onto **Calle Castillo**, (signposted 'Sendero de las Acequias 4h') **(Wp1 0M)**.

From the top of **Calle Castillo**, we climb a mule trail till it crosses the **Acequia de los Castaños (Wp.2, 3M)**, where we bear right on a minor path passing a large reservoir. Thirty metres after the reservoir we follow a narrow path on the right, bearing away from the main *acequia* feeding the reservoir.

We then climb slightly alongside a minor *acequia*, passing above the flat, vine-decked roof of a small house, after which we rejoin the larger, concreted **Acequia de los Castaños (Wp.3, 13M)**, which we follow through the woods for the next hour, crossing two dirt tracks **(Wps. 4&5, 20M & 35M)**, before reaching its source in the **Río de Mecina (Wp.6, 75M)**.

For easy strolling, return via the same route, otherwise there's a short extension for an alternative view of the valley. After following the goat tracks on the left bank of the river for fifty metres, we cross back onto the right bank and climb to join a broad, partially overgrown track that continues climbing steeply to an eroded slope next to several dead chestnuts.

After bearing right at the chestnuts, we zigzag up across abandoned terraces to join a dirt track **(Wp.7, 90M)**. Turning left, we follow this track, ignoring a minor branch on the left 100 metres later, until we reach a small *cortijo* with a large threshing circle **(Wp.8, 100M)** behind which there's a major junction of dirt tracks.

We turn left again and descend to a stand of oaks where the track bears right **(Wp.9, 105M)**. Leaving the main track, we descend along a minor,

waymarked branch to the left, passing behind twin threshing circles (still in use), a small cabin and an ancient threshing machine.

The path descends steeply to another *cortijo* with waymarks on a corner of the main building, behind which it crosses a watercourse and climbs slightly to a byre/*cortijo* and a large oak with a deep cleft in the trunk. After crossing another muddy watercourse, we bear left below a small *acequia*.

Following the main tracks, we pass a tiny stone ruin and two small cabins, the second of which has a red and yellow oil barrel by the door. Bearing left at a Y-junction just after the barrel, we descend across a couple of terraced wheat fields where the path disappears. On the right of the lower terrace, a rough access path rejoins the **Acequia de Castaños (W.10, 115M)**, forty minutes from **Mecina-Bombarón**.

Short Version

Turning back at **Wp.6** - 1 hour 15 mins (one-way) / Exertion 1

- GPS Waypoints are provided for each of the 34 detailed route descriptions in **34 Alpujarras Walks** . The waypoint numbers in these lists correspond to the numbers quoted in each walk description, and are for the direction in which Charles Davis describes the route.

- When inputting GPS Waypoints to your GPS receiver, do make sure that you have set the datum to European 1979.

- Note that not all GPS Waypoints are shown on the maps, and those that are shown are placed alongside the route rather than at the exact location.

- GPS Waypoint Navigation using these waypoints is intended to compliment the walk descriptions in 34 Alpujarras Walks, it is not a replacement for accurate walk descriptions or for using the Alpujarras Tour & Trail Map.

- While we quote GPS Waypoints to 0.0001, in practice 0.010 (10 metres) is an acceptable standard of accuracy. GPS Waypoints are extremely difficult to reproduce exactly while on a walking route, unless you spend some time at each waypoint location finding the exact position at which Charles was holding the GPS unit; hence the 10 metre accuracy for reproducing waypoints in the field or on the mountain.

- **GPS - The Easy Way** by David Brawn, is an easy to read guide to getting the best from your hand held GPS unit which takes you from Novice to Expert status in a series of easy to follow exercises. Whether you are just thinking of buying a GPS, if you are a GPS novice or an experienced user, **GPS - The Easy Way** is essential reading.

- **Personal Navigator Files** (**PNF**s) are available for **34 Alpujarras Walks**. **PNF**s comprise the edited Track Log files and Waypoint files prepared from Charles Davis' GPS records of his research for **34 Alpujarras Walks**. See Discovery Walking Guides websites for more information:

www.walking.demon.co.uk and **www.dwgwalking.co.uk**

Walk 1 GR7: Lanjarón-Cáñar-Soportújar (10km 3.5hrs)					
1	36 55.2373	03 28.1498	10	36 55.3987	3 26.5682
2	36 55.1647	03 28.0550	11	36 55.6459	3 26.4452
3	36 55.2091	3 27.9482	12	36 55.7077	3 26.4362
4	36 55.2571	3 27.8432	13	36 55.9375	3 26.3654
5	36 55.2565	3 27.6650	14	36 55.7875	3 26.1357
6	36 55.1104	3 27.4797	15	36 55.7689	3 25.8609
7	36 55.1419	3 27.1208	16	36 55.6675	3 25.6665
8	36 55.3111	3 26.7014	17	36 55.6585	3 25.4739
9	36 55.3531	3 26.6084	18	36 56.3761	3 24.7893
			19	36 56.5411	3 24.6531
			20	36 56.4397	3 24.5955

21	36 56.0155	3 24.5031
22	36 55.9321	3 24.4491
23	36 55.8619	3 24.4041
24	36 55.7977	3 24.3495
25	36 55.5463	3 24.4137
26	36 55.3189	3 24.6579

Walk 2 GR7: Soportújar-Pampaneira (6km 2hrs)

1	36 55.6507	3 23.8557
2	36 55.6027	3 23.4531
3	36 55.6297	3 23.3391
4	36 55.5079	3 23.1699
5	36 55.5403	3 23.0451
6	36 55.7209	3 22.6245
7	36 56.0059	3 22.4205
8	36 56.3839	3 21.9531
9	36 56.6131	3 21.7623
10	36 56.5855	3 21.6309

Walk 3 GR7: Bubión-Pitres-Bubion (8km 2.5hrs)

1	36 56.9359	3 21.1653
2	36 56.6791	3 21.0699
3	36 56.5093	3 21.0153
4	36 56.4631	3 20.9205
5	36 56.3899	3 20.7207
6	36 56.4936	3 20.1105
7	36 56.4480	3 20.0007
8	36 56.4780	3 19.7235
9	36 56.3046	3 19.5831
10	36 56.6334	3 19.7733

Walk 4 GR7: Busquístar-Trevéelez (9km 4hrs)

1	36 56.3976	3 17.6086
2	36 56.4612	3 17.4016
3	36 56.5620	3 17.3290
4	36 57.0990	3 17.1790
5	36 57.1422	3 17.0896
6	36 57.4884	3 17.3818
7	36 57.9048	3 17.1460
8	36 58.0692	3 17.3272
9	36 58.6440	3 17.0602
10	36 59.0496	3 17.2047
11	36 59.2644	3 17.3289
12	36 59.3034	3 17.1285
13	36 59.2446	3 16.8039
14	36 59.3466	3 16.8303
15	36 59.6946	3 16.4175
16	37 00.0096	3 16.3329
17	37 00.1674	3 16.3227
18	37 00.2874	3 16.1577

Walk 5 GR7: Trevélez-Juviles (7km 2hrs)

1	37 00.0330	3 15.6802
2	36 59.9190	3 15.5596
3	36 59.5728	3 15.6862
4	36 59.3898	3 15.6322
5	36 58.5660	3 15.5752
6	36 58.2222	3 15.4798
7	36 57.8166	3 15.2566
8	36 57.7872	3 15.1582
9	36 57.7686	3 14.8546
10	36 57.3876	3 13.7740
11	36 57.2478	3 13.5250
12	36 56.9838	3 13.4632

Walk 6 GR7: Juviles-Cádiar, plus optional loop between Cádiar and Lobras. Juviles-Cádiar (8km 2.5hrs) Cádiar-Lobras (7km 2hrs) Lobras-Cádiar loop (10km 3hrs)

1	36 57.0660	3 13.3744
2	36 57.0990	3 12.9418
3	36 56.9574	3 12.6076
4	36 56.7798	3 12.5704
5	36 56.5206	3 12.8842
6	36 56.3010	3 12.9353
7	36 56.0406	3 12.8117
8	36 55.9416	3 12.8009
9	36 55.5834	3 12.6113
10	36 55.5762	3 12.2999
11	36 55.6512	3 11.9357
12	36 55.6380	3 11.6201
13	36 55.6968	3 11.4257
14	36 55.8558	3 11.1257
15	36 55.4468	3 10.7873
16	36 55.8008	3 10.8575
17	36 55.8936	3 10.6187
18	36 55.7784	3 10.5875
19	36 55.4946	3 10.9247
20	36 55.2570	3 11.5463
21	36 55.0758	3 11.9327
22	36 54.9816	3 12.2639
23	36 54.8820	3 12.4811
24	36 54.9312	3 12.6443
25	36 55.9242	3 12.3581
26	36 55.9002	3 12.6833

Walk 7 GR7: Cádiar-Bérchules-Mecina-Bombarón (9km 3hrs)

1	36 56.7066	3 10.7477
2	36 56.9052	3 10.8605
3	36 57.4283	3 10.7459
4	36 57.5237	3 10.7555
5	36 57.7289	3 11.2031
6	36 57.7643	3 11.3393
7	36 57.9767	3 11.3770
8	36 58.7801	3 11.3260
9	36 59.1197	3 11.1898
10	36 59.0441	3 10.8976
11	36 58.7363	3 10.7668
12	36 58.6781	3 10.3691
13	36 58.9955	3 09.3977

Walk 8 GR142: Lobras-Busquístar (11km 4hrs)

1	36 55.6872	3 12.6347
2	36 55.4730	3 13.4759
3	36 55.5582	3 13.6834
4	36 55.9278	3 13.5940
5	36 56.0748	3 13.7830
6	36 55.9764	3 15.1432
7	36 55.8450	3 15.4654
8	36 55.3422	3 15.7732
9	36 55.0494	3 16.5214
10	36 55.6038	3 16.9972
11	36 55.6878	3 17.2126
12	36 56.0118	3 17.3404
13	36 56.2626	3 17.5870

Walk 9 GR142: Órgiva-Lanjarón (6km 2hrs)

1	36 54.2269	3 25.4955
2	36 54.1963	3 25.6245
3	36 54.2845	3 25.8357
4	36 54.2353	3 25.9119
5	36 54.3703	3 25.9749
6	36 54.8299	3 26.1045
7	36 54.9469	3 26.4783
8	36 55.0147	3 26.5767
9	36 55.0465	3 26.8923
10	36 55.1155	3 27.1316
11	36 55.0399	3 27.5444
12	36 55.0711	3 27.8420
13	36 54.9439	3 28.1978
14	36 55.2145	3 28.1516

Walk 10 Bayacas-Órgiva-Bayacas (5km 2hrs)

1	36 55.2223	3 24.8307
2	36 55.3285	3 24.6489
3	36 54.6367	3 25.1061
4	36 54.4237	3 25.3215
5	36 54.3385	3 25.4241
6	36 54.3865	3 25.4745
7	36 54.6427	3 25.4457
8	36 54.6907	3 25.5309
9	36 54.8029	3 25.5531
10	36 54.9019	3 25.4421
11	36 55.0615	3 25.2753
12	36 55.0699	3 25.1541

Walk 11 Camino de la Sierra: Lanjarón-Puente El Vadillo & Casa Forestal de Tello (8km 3.5-4hrs)

1	36 55.3267	3 28.2056
2	36 55.4059	3 28.2476
3	36 55.4977	3 28.2608
4	36 56.1637	3 28.0736
5	36 56.9803	3 27.7658
6	36 57.0469	3 27.7040
7	36 57.2785	3 27.5390
8	36 57.4597	3 27.5552
9	36 57.5797	3 27.6080

Walk 12 El Caballo (9km 5hrs)

1	36 58.5889	3 27.7838
2	36 58.9303	3 27.8012
3	36 59.4565	3 27.4970
4	37 00.2323	3 26.7104
5	37 00.4819	3 26.4260
6	37 00.7908	3 26.3150
7	37 00.9288	3 26.1572
8	37 00.4237	3 26.6684
9	37 00.1879	3 26.8478
10	36 59.4493	3 27.4028
11	36 59.0509	3 27.7358

Walk 13 Cerro Man-Puente Palo (6km 2hrs)

1	36 56.5273	3 25.3953
2	36 56.6401	3 25.4426
3	36 56.8423	3 25.4720
4	36 57.2275	3 25.4396
5	36 57.3145	3 25.3802
6	36 57.5569	3 25.0670
7	36 57.9067	3 24.8792
8	36 58.0447	3 24.7274
9	36 57.3877	3 25.3484

Walk 14 Puente Palo-Pico Alegas-Puente Palo (11km 5.5hrs)

1	36 58.0891	3 24.7166
2	36 58.4653	3 24.6236
3	36 58.5787	3 24.7952
4	36 59.2236	3 24.2156
5	36 59.4528	3 24.1112
6	36 59.3754	3 24.0722
7	36 59.3268	3 24.0386
8	36 59.3520	3 24.0350
9	36 59.3958	3 24.0326
10	36 59.3304	3 23.9960
11	36 59.4180	3 23.9816
12	36 59.4882	3 23.9504
13	36 59.5434	3 23.8898
14	36 59.5518	3 23.8388
15	36 59.4570	3 23.8514
16	36 59.6802	3 23.7650
17	36 59.9532	3 23.4794
18	37 00.1512	3 23.4422
19	36 59.0358	3 23.6930
20	36 58.2295	3 23.5587
21	36 57.8719	3 23.5545
22	36 58.0231	3 24.3998

Walk 15 Poqueira Villages (7km 3hrs)

1	36 56.5477	3 21.4983
2	36 56.9497	3 21.3465
3	36 57.0925	3 21.3885
4	36 57.3936	3 21.4005
5	36 57.5298	3 21.3627
6	36 57.7944	3 21.6171
7	36 58.1814	3 21.7335
8	36 58.0890	3 21.8157
9	36 57.7620	3 22.0395
10	36 57.6678	3 21.9147
11	36 57.5053	3 21.8967
12	36 57.0973	3 21.9909
13	36 56.8837	3 21.8043
14	36 56.8969	3 21.6951
15	36 56.5921	3 21.6363

Walk 16 Pampaneira-Pitres-Pampaneira (12km 4-5hrs)

1	36 56.2561	3 21.6483
2	36 56.4319	3 21.4635
3	36 56.5609	3 21.4293
4	36 56.5387	3 21.2601
5	36 56.4829	3 21.0339
6	36 56.4427	3 20.9385
7	36 56.6964	3 20.7657
8	36 56.3395	3 20.3067
9	36 56.0791	3 20.7273
10	36 56.0917	3 20.3955
11	36 56.0779	3 20.2893
12	36 56.2296	3 19.9599
13	36 56.2194	3 19.8201
14	36 56.2404	3 19.5315
15	36 56.1007	3 21.0939
16	36 56.0293	3 21.1767
17	36 55.9555	3 21.1905
18	36 55.9273	3 21.2685
19	36 55.8493	3 21.6249
20	36 55.9711	3 21.1347

Walk 17 Capileira-La Cebadilla-Capileira (7km 2.5hrs)

1	36 57.8022	3 21.5001
2	36 57.9912	3 21.4497
3	36 58.0632	3 21.3825
4	36 58.2822	3 21.2829
5	36 58.6932	3 21.2445
6	36 59.4492	3 20.9799
7	36 59.2314	3 21.2061
8	36 59.0274	3 21.4395
9	36 58.2522	3 21.7041
10	36 57.8808	3 21.5751

Walk 18 Río Naute circuit (9km 4hrs)

1	36 59.4534	3 20.9787
2	36 59.7018	3 20.9253
3	36 59.7510	3 20.9247
4	36 59.9184	3 20.8509
5	37 00.3144	3 20.4411
6	37 00.3738	3 20.3517
7	37 00.6180	3 20.2245
8	37 00.8112	3 20.0967
9	37 00.9192	3 19.9599
10	37 01.0302	3 20.0637
11	37 01.0668	3 20.1165
12	37 01.1388	3 20.1651
13	37 01.2246	3 20.5551
14	37 00.8712	3 20.4867
15	37 00.8166	3 20.6145
16	37 00.5382	3 21.1401
17	36 59.8764	3 20.9925

Walk 19 La Atalaya & O.Sel.Ling from Bubión (12km 5hrs)

1	36 57.5172	3 21.8409
2	36 57.5059	3 21.8979
3	36 57.6150	3 21.8691
4	36 57.6684	3 21.9159
5	36 57.7488	3 22.0437
6	36 57.6721	3 22.1559
7	36 57.6265	3 22.2459
8	36 57.6625	3 22.2843
9	36 57.6577	3 22.3653
10	36 57.3931	3 22.3593
11	36 57.4501	3 22.5489
12	36 57.1831	3 22.7091
13	36 57.1687	3 22.8537
14	36 56.6407	3 23.0271
15	36 56.4421	3 23.1285
16	36 56.2459	3 23.1411
17	36 56.1439	3 22.9815
18	36 56.5579	3 22.6185
19	36 56.8609	3 22.3719
20	36 57.1435	3 22.2255

21	36 57.1855	3 22.0503
22	36 57.0961	3 21.9903

Walk 20 Poqueira Refuge via the Acequias (14km 5hrs)

1	36 58.4262	3 20.6151
2	36 58.6356	3 20.4777
3	36 59.3208	3 20.1771
4	36 59.7036	3 20.0739
5	36 59.9592	3 19.8423
6	37 01.1562	3 19.7343
7	37 01.2342	3 19.6281
8	37 01.7226	3 19.3539
9	36 59.9880	3 19.7859
10	36 59.7288	3 20.0235
11	36 58.6332	3 20.3973

Walk 21 Mulhacén (8.5hrs 22km)

1	36 58.2245	3 19.9735
2	36 58.6098	3 19.8861
3	36 58.7322	3 19.7721
4	36 59.3490	3 19.6065
5	36 59.5248	3 19.4151
6	37 00.9180	3 18.5865
7	37 01.7220	3 19.3485
8	37 02.3172	3 19.4343
9	37 02.8902	3 19.4066
10	37 03.3245	3 19.4168
11	37 03.3593	3 19.5194
12	37 03.2195	3 18.9645
13	37 03.2789	3 18.6231
14	37 02.7305	3 18.6543
15	37 02.2907	3 18.2169
16	37 00.8658	3 18.1473
17	37 00.6282	3 18.0837

Walk 22 Pórtugos Junta de Los Ríos (5km 2.5hrs)

1	36 56.8062	3 19.0905
2	36 56.9928	3 19.1295
3	36 57.2646	3 19.3227
4	36 57.3858	3 19.4445
5	36 57.4284	3 19.4949
6	36 57.5136	3 19.6035
7	36 57.2808	3 19.7331
8	36 57.2034	3 19.7067
9	36 56.9184	3 19.4151
10	36 56.7162	3 19.3335
11	36 56.5902	3 19.5285
12	36 56.5530	3 19.3281
13	36 56.5230	3 19.1805
14	36 56.4900	3 18.8650

Walk 23 La Tahá 1 (9km 3.5hrs)

1	36 56.3052	3 19.3096
2	36 56.3502	3 19.2334
3	36 56.3136	3 19.0654
4	36 56.1438	3 18.4462
5	36 56.2134	3 18.4570
6	36 56.5200	3 18.6070
7	36 56.3166	3 18.0856
8	36 56.4204	3 17.7118
9	36 56.2656	3 17.6500
10	36 55.9044	3 18.0496
11	36 55.9404	3 18.1246
12	36 56.2164	3 18.0634
13	36 56.1144	3 18.2800

Walk 24 La Tahá (2 5km 2hrs)

1	36 56.1252	3 18.6280
2	36 55.9824	3 18.6892
3	36 55.7958	3 18.7480
4	36 55.7484	3 19.0402
5	36 55.6866	3 19.1068
6	36 55.5654	3 18.9700
7	36 55.7292	3 18.8998
8	36 55.9188	3 18.4702
9	36 55.8996	3 18.3388
10	36 56.0970	3 18.4672
11	36 56.0970	3 18.5446

Walk 25 Sierra Mecina (9km 3hrs)

1	36 55.6175	3 19.2273
2	36 55.0717	3 19.5484
3	36 54.8011	3 19.7974
4	36 55.3686	3 17.8474
5	36 55.6092	3 17.9860
6	36 55.7418	3 17.9722
7	36 55.8936	3 18.3028
8	36 55.9014	3 18.3388

Walk 26 Los Helechones, El Portichuelo de Cástaras and Los Cerillos Negros (8km 3hrs)

1	36 56.3124	3 17.5348
2	36 56.5122	3 17.0644
3	36 56.7210	3 16.8010
4	36 56.7924	3 16.5904
5	36 56.9508	3 16.2694
6	36 57.0618	3 16.1674
7	36 56.7654	3 16.1002
8	36 56.6538	3 16.2466
9	36 56.5680	3 16.5046
10	36 56.3262	3 16.5676

Walk 27 Río Culo Perro (9km 3hrs)

1	37 00.2484	3 15.9093
2	37 00.4644	3 15.9309
3	37 01.1489	3 15.6009
4	37 01.9727	3 15.2865
5	37 02.0927	3 15.2787
6	37 02.1941	3 15.3015
7	37 02.4035	3 15.3867
8	37 02.0885	3 15.0621
9	37 02.1569	3 14.8209
10	37 02.2007	3 14.8425
11	37 02.2079	3 14.7045

Walk 28 Headwaters of the Río Trevélez via the Camino de Granada (14km 4.5hrs)

1	37 00.1330	3 15.8100
2	37 00.3804	3 15.5811
3	37 01.0169	3 15.2007
4	37 01.4333	3 15.1485
5	37 01.5683	3 15.0207
6	37 01.9379	3 14.8677
7	37 02.2079	3 14.7057
8	37 02.8577	3 14.4693
9	37 03.3299	3 14.4249
10	37 03.7889	3 14.4879
11	37 03.9623	3 14.5449

Walk 29 Siete Lagunas (20km 7hrs)

1	37 00.2514	3 15.9081
2	37 01.5017	3 15.8787
3	37 02.0279	3 16.2537
4	37 02.5259	3 16.8969
5	37 02.9033	3 17.3355
6	37 02.9345	3 17.5545
7	37 02.8115	3 17.5449
8	37 02.5067	3 17.6715
9	37 02.1791	3 17.9271
10	37 00.6366	3 18.0177
11	37 00.5280	3 17.3055
12	37 00.2766	3 16.7619
13	37 00.2952	3 16.2969

Walk 30 Trevélez-Peñabón + optional descent to Bérchules (11.5km 5hrs)

1	37 00.0396	3 15.6526
2	36 59.8926	3 15.5620
3	36 59.8398	3 15.5710
4	36 59.7675	3 15.5428
5	36 59.7714	3 15.4354
6	36 59.5932	3 15.2554
7	36 59.7306	3 14.8252
8	36 59.8061	3 14.7244
9	36 59.8619	3 14.5036
10	36 59.8625	3 14.1070
11	37 00.5447	3 14.0434
12	37 00.1883	3 14.3752
13	36 58.7927	3 13.3402
14	36 58.7231	3 13.0402
15	36 58.5935	3 12.7456
16	36 58.4459	3 12.2434
17	36 58.4747	3 12.0640
18	36 58.4771	3 11.5834

Walk 31 Cerro Macilla-Cástaras (4km 2hrs)

1	36 56.7324	3 14.5618
2	36 56.6508	3 14.7088
3	36 56.5980	3 14.8468
4	36 56.5242	3 14.9320
5	36 56.3724	3 15.0292
6	36 56.2044	3 15.1174
7	36 56.0610	3 15.1990
8	36 56.0310	3 15.2104
9	36 56.1564	3 15.3448
10	36 56.1534	3 15.4054
11	36 56.1822	3 15.4612
12	36 56.2368	3 15.4036

13	36 56.3814	3 15.3112
14	36 56.2878	3 15.0856

Walk 32 Bérchules Junta de los Ríos + extension to Hoya del Borrego (10km 3.5hrs)

1	36 58.8305	3 11.3410
2	36 59.1419	3 11.4034
3	36 59.2403	3 11.5084
4	36 59.6057	3 11.7430
5	37 00.1979	3 11.6680
6	37 00.2147	3 11.6896
7	37 00.9029	3 11.1784
8	37 01.4843	3 10.9402
9	37 00.8843	3 11.1142
10	36 59.3891	3 11.6338

Walk 33 Cerro Gordo (15km 6hrs)

1	36 58.6829	3 11.3368
2	36 58.7381	3 10.7644
3	36 59.2565	3 10.7956
4	36 59.2907	3 10.5658
5	36 59.6237	3 10.3744
6	37 00.8201	3 10.3888
7	37 00.4811	3 10.6432
8	37 00.8765	3 10.4092
9	37 01.7825	3 10.4812
10	37 01.8161	3 10.5550
11	37 01.8179	3 10.6474
12	37 01.5089	3 10.9210
13	37 00.9053	3 11.1802
14	37 00.3461	3 11.6278

Walk 34 PRA111 Mecina-Bombarón, Acequia de los Castaños (8km 2.5hrs)

1	36 58.9931	3 09.4181
2	36 59.0507	3 09.4733
3	36 59.2193	3 09.4439
4	36 59.4209	3 09.3215
5	36 59.7443	3 09.1799
6	37 00.7403	3 08.7928
7	37 00.8435	3 08.9506
8	37 00.5585	3 09.0442
9	37 00.4067	3 09.1072
10	37 00.0959	3 08.9987

GLOSSARY

SPANISH WORDS USED IN THE TEXT:

acequia — see introduction

área recreativa — designated picnic spot with tables, benches and barbecues; running water or a spring are optional, large quantities of rubbish virtually obligatory

baños — baths

barranco — a gully, gorge or ravine

cabra montés — mountain goat

cañada — a slightly confusing word this; in low mountains it's generally used to describe the bottom of a gully or ravine, but in high-mountains it more often refers to one of the traditional rights of way (frequently running along the top of a ridge!) used for transhumance or carrying ice down to the cities

cortijo — farm or farmhouse

cerro — translated as a hill, but for anybody coming from Britain, it's a mountain without a real peak

fuente — a spring or water-source

hoya — literally a 'hole', practically a large dell or dale

lavadero — traditional wash-house, usually with stone washboards and deep sinks

loma — translated as hill, hillock or rise, but mostly applied to a long, broad spur between valleys

mirador — a viewing point, usually though not necessarily with some sort of man-made balcony or terrace

puente — bridge

rambla — a dry watercourse or riverbed

tajo — a cliff or escarpment

tinao — a distinctive feature of Alpujarran villages, a large balcony/terrace, sometimes covered, usually built above the street, frequently linking two houses

vereda — path or lane

vivero — a nursery or arboretum

English Language guides:
> Rough Guide

Spanish walking guides:
> Juan Carlos García Gallego - Excursiones por el Sur de España – 1(Desnivel)

The local tourist authority publishes a useful sketch-map (Turismo Alpujarras, Step by Step) of motoring routes and summarising outdoor activities in the region. Available free from LIDER next to the social security office in Órgiva or from Turismo Alpujarra (see Appendix C).

Elma Thompson publishes alternative walking leaflets in English, available from Nevedensis (see below).

Alpujarras books in English:

Gerald Brenan	South From Granada (Penguin)
Chris Stewart	Driving Over Lemons (Sort of Books)
	A Parrot in the Pepper Tree (Sort of Books)

(these three books are widely available in the Alpujarras)

Guides to Flora & Fauna:
Betty Molesworth Allen   Wildflowers of Southern Spain (Santana Books)

Fondo Natural publish a handy series of themed pocket guides (in Spanish) by José Luis Rodríguez, available from Nevedensis (see below).

Books on Spain in general:

Gerald Brenan	The Face of Spain (Penguin)
John Hooper	The Spaniards (Penguin)
Laurie Lee	As I Walked Out One Midsummer's Morning (Norton)
V. S. Pritchett	The Spanish Temper (Greenwood)
Cees Nooteboom	Roads to Santiago (Panther)
Adam Hopkins	Spanish Journeys (Penguin)
Jan Morris	Spain (Penguin)

PISTAS FORESTALES

Pistas Forestales offer visitors to the Alpujarras an excellent experience of the high sierras at minimal effort. Drivers, trail and mountain bike riders are well served by this network of 'official' dirt roads providing adventurous routes at altitude well away from the tarmac. All the pistas were driveable , and their routes accurately plotted, during our research but you should always take care on these off-road routes. Take particular care in winter, when routes may be snow covered, and after/during wet weather.

Mountain bikers should not miss out on these pistas forestales which provide over a 100 kilometres of off-road adventure combining exertion with spectacular scenery. If ascending PF3 there is real danger of altitude sickness; should you start showing symptoms then stop and start slowly descending again.

34 Alpujarras Walks map sections show parts of the Pistas Forestals where these coincide with our walking routes. For full routes of PFs 1-5 you should refer to the **Alpujarras Tour & Trail Map**. During our research we found a number of discrepancies between pistas forestals surveyed by us, and the routes shown on other maps including the official Spanish maps of the region.

PISTA FORESTAL 1 (PF1)
Lanjarón – Refugio Ventura (access to Walk 12)

The definitive high mountain track. Worth driving even if you don't climb to **Caballo** as there are extraordinary views on the way up. NB Ignore the *Camino Cortado* signs above km 13.2. These are permanent fixtures 'just in case'!

The track starts just before km 6 of the A348 at the western end of **Lanjarón**, opposite the park and next to the old bottling plant. Follow the signs for 'Tello'. The first stretch is concreted, but it soon gives way to dirt and very rough dirt at that. However, it's passable and (in the summer of 2002) the higher sections (above km 13.2) had recently being restabilized.

km6.6   **Fuente Pedro Calvo** (the GR7 to **Niguelas** branches off just before the *fuente*)

km13.2   Just above the 3rd meteorological station, turn right for the stroll down to the **Casa Forestal de Tello** (see Walk 11), left for Walk 12, continuing to...

km14.6   ...pass a branch on the left descending to **Niguelas**

km16.7   This is the last broad stretch before the track gets narrower and more 'impressive' – be prepared!

km17.5   There's a sign indicating a chain that no longer seems to be used

km20.2   We pass a 4th meteorological station, shortly before the end of the dirt track.

> **Suggestion for a stroll**
> Take the dirt track climbing through the pine forest. Turn right on the first right-hand branch then right again at the **Acequia Grande** and follow the *acequia* back to the *Área Recreativa*. Also see Walk 13.

> **Suggestion for a stroll**
> Take the narrower track upriver, cross the *cortijo* with goal posts in the garden, then cross the terraces to take a rough path descending to some nice bathing points beside the bridge to the **Cortijo Ballesteros**.

> **Suggestion for a stroll**
> 400 metres from western end of **Puente Palo** *Área Recreativa* (1.2 km from the **Cáñar** junction), several narrow goat paths climb to the right. Take the broadest, northernmost traces nearest the *Área Recreativa*. Climb through the woods, cross the field and turn right onto a dirt track. Leave the dirt track as it bears left at the upper limit of the oak forest and follow the faint cow paths through the broom/furze. Cross the firebreak into the pine woods onto a minor track leading to the main dirt track (Walk 14) back down to the *Área Recreativa*.

> **Suggestion for a stroll**
> Start as per the last stroll, but turn left on the dirt track after the field and follow it down to the junction with the **Cáñar** branch; turn left to return to the start (1.2 km).

PISTA FORESTAL 2 (PF2)
Ermita del Padre Eterno to **Puente Palo**, **El Robledal** & the **Río Lanjarón** below the **Lomas de Cáñar** & **Lanjarón**.

Good condition except for the last stretch which is a bit rocky. Access to Walks 13 & 14 and various strolls (see below).

The track starts opposite the **Ermita del Padre Eterno**. 0.9 km east of the **Soportújar** turning off the gr-421.

At 500 metres it crosses the GR7 (see Walk 2)

km2.4   A branch on the right leads to **O.Sel.Ling Bhuddist Centre** (5 km, visits between 3 and 6 p.m.) – see Walk 19.

km4.3   The tarmac ends and the dirt track starts at a Park Authority building soon after which we turn right at a sign for **Puente Palo**.

km10.8   The track crosses **Puente Palo**; there's a nice plunge pool above the bridge on the left bank of the **Río Chico** (200 metres before **Puente Palo** *Área Recreativa* – see Walk 13)

km11.2   The chained track on the right marks the start of Walk 14

km13   Branch A descends on the left to **Cáñar** and the start of Walk 13. The track on the right climbs into **El Robledal**, the region's finest oak forest.

km13.8   **Casa Forestal de Cáñar**

km15.2   Branch B descends on the left to **Lanjarón**.

km16.3   Branch C descends on the left to **Lanjarón**.

km18.9   Almost the end of the track and a convenient turning point. The main track bears right to climb to some *cortijos*, the narrower track ahead leads towards the bridge to the **Cortijo de Ballesteros**

NB
Beware of improvising circuits via **Ballesteros** and the **Casa Forestal de Tello**; the **Tello** bridge is difficult to find if you don't already know it, it's a very steep climb back up from the lower part of the river, and it generally ends with having to scale a fence! Climb back up from the river by the same path, but bear left away from the terraces to pass behind a large byre with a fenced corral, behind which you'll find a faint track leading to a clear dirt track back to the start.

Branch A
Quite rough but passable. After descending 700 metres, a turning on the left leads to **Cortijo La Muda** (500 metres) currently being restored as a **Casa Rural** (see Fernando Vilchez – useful addresses)

km3.8   The sharp bend just to the **East of Cerro Man** marks the starting point for Walk 13 (8.7 km from **Cáñar**)

Branch B
This is perhaps the most attractive descent with wonderful views of **Cáñar**.

Branch C
There's a couple of gates across this track, but they've always been open when we passed. The following distances are descending.

km0.6   A branch to the right leads down to the **Río Lanjarón** and the top of Walk 11, km 9.1 The track crosses the GR7 (Walk 1, Wp.7) & joins the GR142 (Walk 9, Wp.10).

km12   The track/GR142 joins the road at the eastern end of **Lanjarón** (Walk 1, Wp.1).

PISTA FORESTAL 3 (PF3)
The 'Carretera de Veleta' to Hoya del Portillo (GR411)

A well-maintained track, which will probably continue to be so since it's used by the Park Authority buses. Though it was never fully asphalted, this is still popularly called a *carretera* or 'road' in honour of its initial pretensions, and for some while it was celebrated as the highest road in Europe, crossing the

Sierra Nevada from **Capileira** to **Güéjar-Sierra**

Nowadays though the higher stretches are closed to motorised traffic, thankfully, and the road is gradually being reclaimed for nature, both by her own efforts and those of ecologists. For cyclists and equestrians, the 50 km crossing to the ski station at **Pradollano** remains an attractive excursion, but it makes for pretty dull walking. This description ends at the **Hoya del Portillo** barrier.

Access to Walks 18, 20 & 21, and four strolls (see below and Walk 21).

Set the odometer at zero at the sign for the coach-park ('P Autocares') as you leave **Capileira**.

Suggestion for a stroll

Barranco de Cereza Robledal: park in the large lay-by 700 metres after the coach-park.

NB

The **Bubíon-Cebadilla** wayposted path crosses the road here. Go back down the road 100 metres and take the second dirt track on the left down to the junction with the GR7 (Walk 3, Wp.2). Bear left on the dirt track and stay on the dirt track when the GR7 bears right. Shortly before it ends, leave the dirt track on a clear path to the left marked by a small cairn. Follow the path up to the dirt track to **Pitres/Prado Toro** (see km 1.5 below). Bear left on the track then follow the road back to the car.

km 1.5 Branch on the right signposted 'Cortijo Prado Toro' (see Appendix C, Sleeping), an alternative and more direct car-route to **Pitres**.

Suggestion for a stroll

Peña del Angel. Not everybody's idea of a 'stroll' as the loop at the end involves some fairly athletic clambering about rocks. However, nobody's obliging you to climb, most of the route is on a dirt track, and almost equally breathtaking views can be had from just before the rocks. Follow the branch track to the Y-junction, then bear right and scramble up the rocky pinnacles of the **Peña** before descending at their southern end and following the dirt track back to the car.

Suggestion for a stroll

Tajo de Soju. Essentially a continuation of the last stroll, you could either combine the two or drive past the **Peña del Angel** and park at the junction with the GR7 just after the two abandoned electricity towers. Continue on the dirt track till it ends in a little turning circle then take the path along the ridge and follow the firebreak till it starts to descend, a point that constitutes a natural *mirador* with some of the finest views to be had from anywhere of the **Poqueira Gorge** and the 3000 metre peaks. Especially recommended in winter.

---

km2.7   Branch on the left to **La Cebadilla** (Walk 18)

km3.8   On the right, Pista Forestal 4 to **Trevélez**, signposted 'AR Río Bermejo 3km' km 5   End of asphalt, start of the dirt track

km7.1   Branch on the left to the start of Walk 20

km8.9   The firebreak on the left leads up to **Puerto Molina**, an alternative start to Walk 21 in spring if there's still snow below **Hoya del Portillo**.

km10.4   The barrier at **Hoya del Portillo** – so according to my odometer, it's not 13 km as the sign above **Capileira** claims!

PISTA FORESTAL 4 (PF4)
Capileira – Trevélez

A stony, dusty Pista Forestal, but well stabilised and easy to drive along in spring, summer and autumn. The nearer you get to **Trevélez**, the narrower and more dramatic it becomes, with magnificent views of the **Tahá**, **Loma de Juviles**, and **Peña de los Papos**. NB the 'GR' markings at the start are not 'GR' markings! (see Introduction, Waymarked Paths).

At km3.8 of Pista Forestal 3, set the odometer at 0 and turn right at a sign saying 'Área Recreativa Río Bermejo 3 km'

km1   There's a nice picnic spot on a platform on the right amid small holm oak

km2.5   The bridge over the **Junta de los Ríos** (see Walk 22)

Suggestion for a stroll
Haza del Cerezo (See Walk 22 Extension)

Suggestion for a stroll
Barranco del Jabalí
NB
Path-finding maybe a problem
Take the dirt track (**N**) on the western side of the bridge. Cross the **Río Chorrera** (also worth exploring for some fine bathing pools) and follow the goat tracks along the right bank of the **Jabalí**, climbing above a large chicane in the watercourse before descending to a makeshift dam forming a deep bathing pool. Cross the watercourse and follow the goat tracks south on the left bank of the **Jabalí** up to a dirt track above a goat farm. Take the dirt track back to PF4 and the bridge.

---

km2.7   Branch on the left up to the goat farm mentioned in the last stroll.

km2.9   Turning on the right down to the *Área Recreativa*

Suggestion for a stroll
Wander through the *Área Recreativa* and descend to the bottom of the magnificent waterfall (see Walk 22).

---

km5.4   Branch on the right down to **Pórtugos**

km11.1   Permanently water-logged section (passable at Easter and in summer)

km11.5   Section narrowed by landslip (again passable)

km16.7   Arrive just outside **Trevélez** on the main road into the **Barrios Medio & Alto**.

PISTA FORESTAL 5 (PF5)
Juviles – Mecina-Bombarón

Highly recommended. A remote but well-stabilised track along most of which one can maintain a steady 30/40km an hour. None of our described walks start up here, but there is one stroll and also a route up to the **Peñon del Puerto** marked by cairns. Even if you don't walk though, the track of itself is attractive enough to justify an afternoon's exploration. After about 6 km you start to get a real sense of high-mountain isolation.

If you're coming from the west, the track starts (on the left of the road) 2.6km after **Juviles**. Ignore the branch to the left immediately after you leave the road and, setting the odometer at 0, take the branch climbing on the right.

km2.4   A branch on the right descends to **Bérchules**

km10.5   **Cortijo de Espino**

km11.6   A branch on the left climbs towards the **Loma de Piedra Ventana**

km13   The **Río Chico**

km17   The **Río Grande**

km21.2   A branch on the right follows the firebreak described in Walk 33 down to join the **Mecina-Bombarón** branch (see below). Cairns on the left mark the ascent to **Peñon del Puerto**.

Suggestion for a stroll
Take the firebreak branch on the right and, after 100 metres, join Walk 33 (Wps. 6-8)

---

km23.8   The branch on the right is the main track down to **Mecina-Bombarón**

Staying on the track north, we pass **Fuente de los Correlillo**s (km24.6) shortly after which the track goes off our map. If you want to explore further, it's well worth visiting the tiny but exquisite little *Area Recreativa* at **Las Chorreras** (km28.2). After the **Río de Mecina** (km29.2), the landscape becomes more barren, but there's a nice track descending to the east of **Mecina-Bombarón** from km33.3.

If you're coming from the east, the branch emerging at km23.8, starts 1.8km from the western limits of **Mecina-Bombarón**, from where the following distances are relevant:

km1.6   The track joins the GR7 (Walk 7) and we turn left.

km2.4   The GR7 bears left on a minor track, we bear right.

km5.6   We pass (on our left) the lower end of the firebreak-track from **Cerro Gordo** (see km21.2 above)

km9.9   The track emerges at the km23.8 point mentioned above. Turn left for **Cerro Gordo**, 12.7km from the road.

ADDITIONAL STROLLS

A few extras that didn't really fit in with any of the walks or *pistas forestales* but seemed too good to ignore!

The Río Chico above Bayacas
From **Bayacas** bridge follow the left bank of the **Río Chico (N)**. Pass under the main road bridge and climb to the left of the silt-dam for a pleasant picnic spot and some small plunge pools. If you're feeling more adventurous and energetic, continue up the right bank along rough goat trails littered with fallen trees to a high waterfall and a wilder glade. If you really want to get the blood moving, cross the glade to join a broader path winding up to a junction. Carry straight on for a vertiginous *acequia* path to source OR turn right for a threshing circle with fine views south over the valley and the **Sierra Lújar** and, north, up to **Puente Palo** and the **Loma de Cáñar**.

The Mirador de Poqueira
Hundreds of people stop here everyday, but few realise the views from the little watchtower along the ridge are even more dramatic. To be honest, few even notice the watchtower! 400 metres after the **Pampaneira** Fina station (dir. Pitres) take the rough path from the *mirador* along the ridge to the outcrop of rocks for giddying views of the gorge.

The Acequia de Cuna
A stroll that's also a paddle - providing there's water in the *acequia*; if there isn't the fun is dramatically diminished. We often walk alongside *acequia*s, here we walk IN one. Take your plastic sandals. Ten metres south of the km 23 sign on the **Trevélez-Busquístar** road, directly opposite the metal sign for the **Trevélez** campsite, a tiny path between two young plane trees climbs very steeply for about fifteen metres to the *acequia*. For an easier access, take the path seventy-five metres further south where the road bears right. Follow the *acequia* south to the second large outcrop of rock, beyond which it has been abandoned, becoming increasingly overgrown, eventually petering out after a fence in the **Barranco de la Bina**. Return the same way, taking the alternative access path for an easier descent.

The best swimming pool in the Alpujarras
Two kilometres from the **Trevélez** bridge (dir. Juviles), park in the lay-by just after the **Barranco de los Castaños**. Take the path below the crash barriers before the next bend to descend to the river. At the Y-junction, bear left for a nice picnic/bathing spot under immense poplars, right for a deep swimming pool below the metal footbridge. **NB** don't swim too near the waterfall on the off-chance that some debris might be pitched over.

USEFUL INFORMATION

Telephone numbers, web addresses and recommendations

Though all reasonable care has been taken to ensure the following
information is up-to-date, experience suggests the authorities in Spain
change their phone lines with alarming regularity.

 RESERVATIONS

www.turandalucia.com   www.turgranada.com

www.rusticblue.com   www.hotelandalucia.com

www.associacion.org   www.rusticblue.com

www.spainyoga.com/PropertyRentals.htm www.lanjaron.org

www.descubrealpujarra.com

 Early morning bus Capileira - Mirador de Trevélez
To book a seat on the early morning bus from **Capileira** to the **Mirador de
Trevélez** (see Walk 21)   T: 686 414 576.

See below for hotels with websites

 SLEEPING, EATING AND DRINKING

(RG)   Rough Guide recommendations
T: Telephone   (The code for Spain is 34)
F: Fax

Lanjarón
(RG) Hotel España   T/F: 958 770 187
(RG) Apartamentos Castillo
        Aladima   T: 958 770 809
                                          www.alcadima.com
(RG) Bar/Hostal Galvez   T: 958 770 702
(RG) Restaurante Manolete, Calle
Queipo de Llano, Hotel Nuevo   T: 958 770 773
Manolete, Calle San Sebastián   www.lanjaron.org

Órgiva
Hotel Taray   T: 958 784 525
                                          www.paginas-
                                          amarillas.es/on/line/htaray

(RG) Hostal/Restaurante Alma
        Alpurrajeña   T: 958 784 085
(RG) Hostal Mirasol   T: 958 785 159
(RG) Bar/Restaurante El Semáforo

Cáñar
Fernando Vilchez T: 696 89 47 99. Has a fine apartment to rent in **Cáñar** (36 euros a day) and is currently restoring **Cortijo La Muda**, near **Puente Palo**, where he'll rent rooms (ideally placed for a three day excursion from **Cáñar** to **Pico Alegas**, see Walks 13 & 14). No English, but he does speak perfect French. He's also an agent for guided walks and paragliding and is willing to act as a landrover taxi.

María Domínguez Pérez / José Alvarez Guerrero T: 958 785 306 / 958 784 444 / 630 482 371. They hold one of the local bars and have houses to rent near **Puente Palo**.

Soportújar
(RG) Bar/Hostal Correillo, Calle Real	T: 958 787 578	
Mirador de Boabdil	T: 958 785 055	F:958 784 965

Carataunas
(RG) El Montañero   T: 958 787 528
www.hotelmontanero.com (part owned by Elma Thompson - see bibliography) (see Walk 1)

Pampaneira
Hostal/Bar/Restaurante Guillerm.   T: 958 763 023
A must for carnivores. The black pudding is extraordinary.
(See Walk 2)
Hostal/Restaurante Casa Diego, Plaza de la Libertad	T:958 763 102
Hostal Ruta del Mulhacén	T: 958 763 010
Pensión/Restaurante Pampaneira	T:958 763 002

Bubíon
(RG) Pensión/Apartamentos Las Terrazas	T: 958 763 034
Villa Turística	T: 958 763 909
www.villabubion.com
(RG) Restaurante La Artesa, Calle Carretera

Capileira
(RG) Méson/Hostal Poqueira	T/F: 958 763 048	
Fonda/Restaurante El Tilo	T:958 763 048	
Finca Los Llanos	T: 958 763 071	F: 958 763 206
Poqueira Refuge (see Walks 18/20/21)	T: 958 343 349	
Apartamentos Vista Veleta	T: 958 763 070 (see Walk 15)	

La Tahá
Pitres: Hotel San Roque	T: 958 857 528
Refugio de los Albergues	T: 958 766 004
Apartamentos Posada La Tahá	T:958 343 041
Cortijo Prado Toro	T: 958 343 240
www.pradotoro.com   (see Walk 3)
Pórtugos: Hostal Mirador	T: 958 766 014
Busquístar: Hostal Mirador de la Alpujarra	T/F: 958 857 470
Casa Sonia sonia@teleline.es	T/F: 958 857 528

Ferreirola: Sierra y Mar   T: 958 766 171
www.sierraymar.com

Mecina: Hotel Albergue de Mecina   T: 958 766 254   F: 958 766 255
www.hotelalberguedemecina.com

Trevélez
Alcazaba de Busquístar   T: 958 858 687
www.alpujarralcazaba.com
(RG) Hotel La Fragua   T: 958 858 626 /
                         958 858 573   F: 958 858 614
Pensíon Regina   T: 958 858 564

Cástaras
Pensíon Maria   T: 958 855 547

Juviles
(RG) Fonda/Restaurante
        Bar Fernandez   T: 958 769 030
Pensíon Tino   T: 958 769 174

Bérchules
El Halcón   T:958 768 733
Hotel los Bérchules   T: 958 852 530   F: 958 769 00
hot.berchules@interbook.net
(RG) La Posada   T/F: 958 852 541
(RG) Fonda/Restaurante Carayol   T: 958 769 092

Cádiar
Apartamentos Sitio de Estar El Cadi   T: 958 850 469
Apartamentos Ruta de la Alpujarra   T: 958 768 059
Hostal Alquería de Morayma   T: 958 343 221
www.alqueriamorayma.com
                           (see Walk 6)
(RG) Hostal Montoro   T: 958 768 068

Mecina-Bombarón
Apartamentos Mirador de Avellano   T: 958 131 498
Los Molinos   T: 858 851 076
www.arrakis.es/-molinos
Casas Blancas   T: 958 851 151
www.casasblancas.es.vg
www.casasblancas.turincon.com

Bayacas
El Bancal   T: 958 784 595/958 785 579
www.spainyoga.com/
                     PropertyRentals.htm

Campsites

Órgiva   T: 958 784 307
www.perso.wanadoo.es/
campingorgiva
Pitres   T/F: 958 766 111
Trevélez   T/F: 958 858 735
www.teleline.es/personal/cam-trev/camping.htm

Supermarkets

Supermarkets are small and varied; some are awful, some very good. The best we found are La Depensa next to the tobacconist in **Órgiva**, and El Molino, **Busquístar**. The Komo-Komo in **Bubíon**, Spar and Coviran in **Trevélez** and Supermercado in **Alcútar** are OK, too. For cheal bulk purchases try Dia in **Órgiva**.

Buses

| Alsina Graells, the main bus company | T: 958 185 480 www.alsinagraells.es |
| La Tahá Bus, the local company | T: 950 510 800 |

Taxis

Getting a taxi can be a challenge. If the harvest needs bringing in, something more lucrative turns up, or the driver's simply busy in a bar, service may be suspended. At the same time, restaurant owners and complete strangers have been known to offer lifts to stranded tourists, and hitching is always an option.

Juan Funes T: 958 785 331 / 619 957 817. Local & landrover taxi based in **Órgiva**. No English, but says he can be contacted through his English speaking friend Eladio at the Hotel Taray (T: 958 784 525). By Alpujarran standards a model of reliability, though sometimes absent in Granada.

The best way of finding transport is to ask on the spot. That said, other taxi numbers you might try, all prefixed with 958, are as follows: in **Bérchules** T: 753061 & 764047; in **Bubíon** T: 763148; **Busquístar** T: 766036; **Cadíar** T: 750029 & 750051 & 750064; **Capileira** T: 763125; **Cástaras** T: 753035; **Lanjarón** T: 770057 & 770097 & 770000 & 770160; **Órgiva** T: 785190 & 785417 & 785131 & 785225; **Pampaneira** T: 763002; **Pitres** T: 766005; **Pórtugos** T: 766006; **Trevélez** T: 858546 & 858537.

Miscellaneous information

| **Nevedensis** local information about the Alpujarras | T: 958 763 127 www.nevednesis.com |

Tourist Offices
| **Lanjarón** | T: 958 770 282 |
| **Pampaneira** | T: 958 763 301 |

Turismo Alpujarra: c/Lora Ramayo
17 / 18400 Órgiva   T: 958 784 484 / F 95
          email: alta-alpujarra@asociacion-tierra.org

Central Tourist office for Andalucia
A pamphlet of local addresses, telephone numbers and festival dates for the Alpujarras is available from:
Tursimo Andaluz SA / Centro Internacional de Turismo de Andalucia /

Crta. Nac. 340 – Cádiz-Málaga, km 189.6 / 29600 Marbella.

	T: 952 838 785 F: 952 836 369

Sierra Nevada
        Administrative Centre   T: 958 026 300   F: 958 026 310
National Park Visitors
        Centres (weekends)   T: 958 340 625 / 958 763 127
Spain's national parks website   www.mma.es/parques

GR142 information
For detailed information and updates
about the GR142 - Paco   T: 958 784 340

GR7 information
For detailed information and updates
about the GR7 - Jesus Espinosa   T: 659 109 662
(if you can't get through, contact him at the Nevedensis office)

 Spa

Lanjarón Spa (balneario):   T: 958 770 137   F: 958 771 070
     www.aguadelanjaron.es

 Horse riding

Horse-riding from **Trevélez**
Rutas a Caballo   T: 958 858 601

 Bookshops

For a small but carefully chosen selection of books in English, try Atenea
on Calle Lora Tamayo (behind the bus stop) in **Órgiva**.

Maps and walking books (mainly in Spanish) at Nevedensis in
Pampaneira.

 Weather information

National Meteorological Institute   T: 906 365 365
Local long-range forecasts are posted outside the Nevedensis office in
Pampaneira

Emergencies

Emergency co-ordination
        centre Andalucía   T: 112
Emergency Civil Guard   T: 062
Red Cross   T: 913 354 545
Casa de Socorro   T: 958 770 002 (local medical
emergencies)

DISCOVERY WALKING GUIDES

34 WALKS

- a series of Walking Guide Books

We receive praise for our regional walking guide titles in almost every post. Thanks to the many happy users of these guides, DWG has acquired an enviable reputation for interesting and accurately described, walking routes. Now the time is right for our new **34 Walks** series of walking guide books. These new books are wider ranging than our previous guides, covering whole islands or regions. All the routes have been newly researched and even our 'classic' routes have been re-walked and rewritten to ensure that they are up-to-date.

Each title in the **34 Walks** series is designed to provide a wide range of interesting routes for moderately fit walkers, plus some routes for experienced walkers. Thanks to the feedback we receive from walkers we have designed these books so that you have the best walking guide book for the destination. Features in **34 Walks** books include:-

- walking route summary
- fully detailed walk descriptions including frequent timings
- GPS Waypoints (grid references) for all key points on a route
- detailed map at 1:25,000 or 1:40,000 scale for every walking route
- full GPS Waypoint lists for all the walking routes

Add in useful background information, and you have the best value walking guides that you can buy.

34 Walks books form one part of DWG's complete walking package. For each title there is also a **Tour & Trail Map**, or **Walkers' Maps** to complement each book.

Available from good book shops or by mail order. For up to date information on Discovery Walking Guides publications write to DWG Ltd, 10 Tennyson Close, Northampton NN5 7HJ, England or visit:-
www.walking.demon.co.uk or
www.dwgwalking.co.uk

DISCOVERY WALKING GUIDES

TRAIL & TRAIL 1:40,000 SCALE MAPS

Tour & Trail Maps were developed to meet the needs for accurate and up-to-date maps for destinations covered by Discovery Walking Guides. At the core of each **T&T** map design is a comprehensive ground-level survey carried out by car and on foot. The survey results are then translated into DWG's design programme, to produce a digital vector graphic database involving the organisation of several million pieces of information across a large number of 'layers' drawn digitally within our computers. Once a DWG digital vector graphic database has been established, new developments such as new roads and tracks, can be quickly incorporated into the correct layer of the database. Rapid updating, combined with state of the art 'file to plate' pre-press operation, enables DWG to produce new editions of **Tour & Trail Maps** quickly and efficiently.

Tour & Trail Maps have a Latitude/Longitude grid and datum information making them GPS compatible. DWG walking routes are clearly highlighted on **T&T** maps, along with their GPS Waypoints wherever space allows.

From 2003, all new **Tour & Trail Maps** titles will be produced on a super-durable material which is waterproof and tear-proof, making **T&T** maps the toughest maps available, in addition to being the most accurate and up-to-date.

Tour & Trail Maps are available for:-

- **Alpujarras**

- **Madeira**

- **La Gomera**

- **Gran Canaria Mountains**

- **Mallorca North & Mountains**

- **Menorca**

WALKERS' MAPS

New to accompany our **34 Walks** series of guide books is a series of **Walkers' Maps** at a 1:25,000 scale, 4cms = 1km, a scale that is so popular for UK walking.

The interesting walking regions for destinations such as Lanzarote and Tenerife form pockets around the island, and a whole island **Tour & Trail Map** would not be viable; Tenerife at 1:40,000 scale would make a 3 metres by 2 metres map and Lanzarote would only be a bit smaller. Just try unfolding something that size while out on a walking route!

To solve the problem of providing top quality mapping at a pocketable size, we have developed **Walkers' Maps** which bring together the walking regions at 1:25,000 scale onto a single folded map at a size to fit your pocket. This gives you large scale maps for all the routes in a **34 Walks** guide book in one map product.

Tenerife Walkers' Maps will consist of 1:25,000 map sections covering routes in the South (4 map sections), West (one large map section), Las Cañadas/Teide (3 map sections) and the North (one large map section) plus an island locator map. The full **Tenerife Walkers' Map** and **Lanzarote Walkers' Map** are published in two editions; a low cost Paper edition and a Super-Durable waterproof and tearproof edition, using the same materials and techniques as for **Indestructible Maps**.

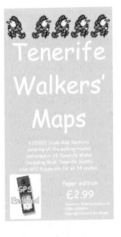

Tenerife Walkers' Maps

1:25,000 Scale Map Sections covering all the walking routes contained in 34 Tenerife Walks (including Walk Tenerife South) plus GPS Waypoints for all 34 routes

Paper edition
£2.99

DISCOVERY WALKING GUIDES

DRIVE! TOURING MAPS

Drive! Touring Maps are designed for today's drivers with the emphasis on accuracy and clarity. Using the digital vector graphic databases from our **Tour & Trail Maps**, plus specially commissioned surveys, **Drive! Touring Maps** are completely up to date on publication. Being up to date is important as Spain has recently changed its road numbering system, which makes driving very confusing if using an old map.

Special design criteria have been developed which result in exceptional clarity, while emphasising the motorist's needs for quick recognition of junctions, road numbers, petrol stations and refreshment stops with off-road parking.

Each **Drive! Touring Map** includes:-
- a comprehensive Place Name Index
- a Distance Chart for main destinations
- datum and grid information enabling the map to be used with modern GPS equipment

All this is backed up by:-
- large scale Street Plans which include Place Names Indexes for major resorts

Drive! Touring Maps include everything you need for exploring these exciting destinations by car.
Drive Touring Maps are available, or in development (D) for:-

- **Tenerife**

- **Lanzarote**

- **La Gomera** (D)

- **Gran Canaria** (D)

- **Fuerteventura** (D)

- **La Palma** (D)

- **Madeira**

- **Mallorca** (D)

- **Menorca**

DISCOVERY WALKING GUIDES

PERSONAL NAVIGATOR FILES

Getting lost is not a pleasant experience, while getting lost in a foreign destination can be distinctly unpleasant. DWG have an excellent reputation for accurately researched and described walking routes, but even we can go further with our revolutionary **Personal Navigator Files**.

All DWG's **34 Walks** series of books are researched using modern GPS equipment, giving us an accuracy of better than five metres. GPS gives us extremely accurate walking routes, and DWG knows exactly where our authors have walked. Now we are making this GPS Track and Waypoint information available for GPS users in a range of formats to suit popular GPS software such as Oziexplorer, GPSY, Fuginawa.

If you have a GPS, download lead and GPS software for your PC, then DWG's new **Personal Navigator Files** will mean that you can follow in the exact footsteps of our walking authors; now that really is 'vorsprung technik' for walkers.

Personal Navigator Files are available for:-

- **Alpujarras**

- **Tenerife**

- **Lanzarote**

- and will be available for all new **34 Walks** destinations. For more information, see DWG websites:-

www.walking.demon.co.uk
and
www.dwgwalking.co.uk

THE INDESTRUCTIBLE MAP COMPANY

INDESTRUCTIBLE MAPS

We've all suffered from maps that fall apart, split down the folds, and soak up water like a sponge. Sellotape, or better drafting tape, is pressed into service to repair the ailing paper map to try and make it last a bit longer. At DWG we believe in durability but even we admit that our paper maps have a limited life when subjected to the rigours of outdoors adventuring. So putting our money where our mouth is, we have formed **The Indestructible Map Company Ltd (TIMCo)**, which does exactly what it says in the name; it produces **Indestructible Maps** which are 'Guaranteed for Life'.

TIMCo combines DWG's expertise in researching and designing the best maps, with the latest materials technology and printing techniques, to produce the **Indestructible Map**. They tell us that the material is a 'high density polymer' core to which they fuse a printable layer of a China Clay type compound; well, they lost us somewhere around 'density' but we do know that what we have got is a map that in 'normal' use will last you a lifetime. It is waterproof, tear-proof, and just about proof to everything apart from fire and attack with sharp objects. You can fold it into a rain hat or beer glass - we've tried, so we know it works - and then still use it as the best map. It feels like silk but appears to have the strength of carbon fibre. You get all of these attributes in an **Indestructible Map** and all at a ridiculous price of £4.99.

Indestructible Maps are not easy to produce - otherwise all map publishers would be using these materials and techniques. Paper is easy. It has been around for hundreds of years and printing paper has been highly developed, plus paper is cheap. Specially coated high density polymer is expensive, eye-wateringly expensive. Printers don't like polymers; they have to run their machines more slowly (more expense), use special inks (very expensive) and put special dryers between each stage of the printing process.

On the first print run of **Tenerife Indestructible Map** our printers forgot some of the complex settings and 455 copies of **Tenerife Indestructible Map** fused themselves into a solid indestructible lump; unfortunately the printers dumped the mistake or we might have been short-listed for the Turner prize!

After all this, you have a lovely **Indestructible Map** as a flat sheet, but that is not the end of your problems. Folding an Indestructible material is a real problem as it always remembers that it once was a flat sheet; TIMCo have to keep the boxes of printed maps sealed until use otherwise we have a lot of flat maps which were once folded!

Enough of the moans and whinges about producing **Indestructible Maps** - just try one for yourself. We are convinced that TIMCo is the future of maps, and we will be using these materials and techniques for DWG's new **Tour & Trail Maps** and **Walkers' Maps**.

www.indestructiblemap.co.uk

WALKING IN THE CANARY ISLANDS

TENERIFE

Despite its 'tabloid' image Tenerife has some of the best walking routes and is suitable for a wide range of walking abilities, up to the most experienced mountain walkers. Once away from the tourist resorts and urban areas, walkers are rewarded with an extensive network of trails and *pistas* on which to explore the unspoilt landscapes. High altitude walking - 2,200 to 3,700 metres altitude - is available in the Las Cañadas/Mount Teide national park. The south and west of the island offer spectacular walking routes combined with easy access from the resorts, as does the upper Orotava Valley in the north. Further afield, the isolated Anaga peninsula will reward walkers prepared to make the long drive from the resorts.

Publications available :-
* **34 Tenerife Walks**
* **Walk Tenerife South**
* **Tenerife Walkers' Maps**
* **Tenerife Indestructible Map**
* **Drive! Tenerife Touring Map**

LA GOMERA

This national heritage island is a walking paradise with spectacular routes in all regions of La Gomera. Garajonay laurel forest is at the island's heart surrounded by huge *barrancos* offering walkers some of the best walking routes in the Canary Islands. Valle Gran Rey and Playa Santiago are developing as resorts but the rest of the island has been blissfully overlooked and offers the rural idyll many seek, if you are prepared for the laborious journey of a flight to Tenerife, transfer to Los Cristianos for ferry to La Gomera; best to book for two weeks or more to make the most of your time on our favourite island.

Publications available :-
* **34 La Gomera Walks**
* **La Gomera Tour & Trail Map**
* **Drive! La Gomera Touring Map**

LA PALMA

Spectacular La Palma is becoming better known, thanks to direct flights from Manchester and Gatwick, plus recent TV programmes. The world's steepest island rises direct from the sea to the high *cumbre* which forms the rim of the Taburiente. The island government has recently installed new waymarking posts and signs covering a wide range of routes. Very rewarding walking for the fitter walker.

LANZAROTE

The fire island is becoming more popular with leisure walkers. Despite having nothing over 700 metres in height, the desert and volcanic landscape contains a surprising variety of walking experiences. Escape from the intensively developed resorts and you will discover landscapes of a barren grandeur, plus a surprising variety of endemic plant life.

Publications available :-
- **34 Lanzarote Walks**
- **Lanzarote Walkers' Maps**
- **Lanzarote Indestructible Map**
- **Drive! Lanzarote Touring Map**

GRAN CANARIA

The best walking is some distance from the southern resorts, centred around Roque Nublo in the centre of the island and stretching westwards. Tremendous scenery amongst the massive canyons combines with a good network of trails to reward adventurous walkers.

Publications available :-
- **Gran Canaria Mountains Tour & Trail Map**
- **Gran Canaria Indestructible Map**
- **Drive Gran Canaria Touring Map**

EL HIERRO

The smallest and least known Canary Island has some of the most varied landscapes of any of the seven islands. Known to ancient mariners as the edge of the known world, it was once the home of the International Meridian which can still be seen on the western tip, before its move to Greenwich. Tiresome plane and ferry transfers mean that El Hierro has been overlooked by mass tourism, giving the island a Shangri-La quality for whose seeking peace and tranquillity. Interesting walking among varied landscapes far from the tourism crowds.

FUERTEVENTURA

'Strong Wind Island' is famous for its huge beaches, windsurfing and naturism. Most barren of the Canary Islands, there is little life outside of the resorts and island capital of Puerto Rosario. A few reasonable walking routes but generally this is an island more suited to Jeep Safari than walking.

Publications available :-
- **Fuerteventura Indestructible Map**
- **Drive! Fuerteventura Touring Map**

GPS THE EASY WAY

Are you are wondering what GPS is? Are you thinking of buying a GPS? Do you wonder what GPS could do for you? Or perhaps you have a GPS and feel it isn't all you thought it would be?

David Brawn's **GPS The Easy Way** will show you what you can do with a GPS. Written in the lively style of DWG and lavishly illustrated, David's book takes you through all aspects of GPS usage from absolute basics up to GPS Expert and debunking the myths about GPS along the way.

'A compass can only point north'

but

'A GPS tells you where you are, where you have been, and can show you where you want to go'.

Essential reading for anyone who wishes to navigate outdoors anywhere in the World.

GPS THE EASY WAY
by
David Brawn

a **DWG** publication

INDEX OF PLACE NAMES